BAD ARTIST

BAD ARTIST

Creating in a Productivity-Obsessed World

Edited by Nellwyn Lampert, Pamela Oakley,
Christian Smith, and Gillian Turnbull

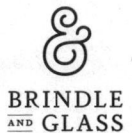

BRINDLE
AND GLASS

Brindle & Glass
An imprint of TouchWood Editions
touchwoodeditions.com

Copy edited by Senica Maltese
Proofread by Marial Shea
Interior design by Sydney Barnes
Cover design by David Drummond

CATALOGUING DATA AVAILABLE FROM LIBRARY AND ARCHIVES CANADA
ISBN 9781990071256 (softcover)
ISBN 9781990071263 (electronic)

TouchWood Editions acknowledges that the land on which we live and work is within the traditional territories of the Lkwungen (Esquimalt and Songhees), Malahat, Pacheedaht, Scia'new, T'Sou-ke and W̱SÁNEĆ (Pauquachin, Tsartlip, Tsawout, Tseycum) peoples.

We acknowledge the financial support of the Government of Canada through the Canada Book Fund and the Canada Council for the Arts, and of the Province of British Columbia through the British Columbia Arts Council and the Book Publishing Tax Credit.

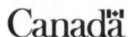 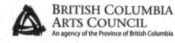 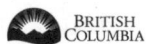

This book was printed using FSC®-certified, acid-free papers, processed chlorine free, and printed with soya-based inks.

Printed in Canada

28 27 26 25 24   1 2 3 4 5

We dedicate this anthology to our dear friend,
Mary Jane Grant, our thankfully not-so-silent partner.

And to those who continue to make art in the face of it all.

CONTENTS

We live in capitalism, its power seems inescapable—but then, so did the divine right of kings. Any human power can be resisted and changed by human beings. Resistance and change often begin in art. Very often in our art, the art of words.

—*Ursula K. Le Guin*

Introduction

"Art without commerce is a hobby."

These words, spoken with much authority to a group of senior fine arts majors, are the kind that those who create art are unable to ignore. We fret over this idea—the thrum of this judgment never far from our thoughts—that if we are not engaged in commerce, then we are not professional; and if we are not professional, can we even call ourselves artists? Art of any form, by its very nature, cannot or should not be quantified, and yet writers measure pages and words; visual artists measure canvases completed; fibre artists measure pieces created all in an effort to appear "productive," to perhaps justify this impulse to create. The notion of creating for art's sake is then seen as hopelessly romantic and nearly indefensible. Of course one can engage in art, but it better be for money, for that is the only marker of success. But was that professor's pronouncement nothing more than an old, tenured windbag parroting the cultural norms and expectations that had, in fact, deemed him "successful"? In Western culture, it is almost impossible to separate professional from commercial, and so the artist is legitimized—distinguished from the hobbyist—by their ability to earn money. Professional art, then, is inherently capitalist.

The *Bad Artist* editors met in a different university arts

classroom some years later. We belonged to different generational cohorts, had jobs ranging from waitress to research scientist, and had completely different reasons for wanting to pursue what is arguably one of the strangest academic honours: a Master of Fine Arts. Despite these differences, the ability to enrol in the MFA at the University of King's College showed us that we had a few things in common: notably, we were privileged enough to exist in a sphere in which pursuing graduate work in creative writing was financially, practically, and systemically possible. Furthermore, entry into the program, regardless of our individual goals, implied a commitment to engage with our creative work in a professional context at least to some degree. And to that end, we have mostly "succeeded," if success is measured in terms of contracts and remuneration. Some of us have traditionally published books, others have used their degree to land teaching jobs, none of us, though, is able to live off our art specifically, thus begging the question: How do we live for art if art can't support our ability to live? More importantly, is that even the right question to ask?

This anthology seeks to be an antidote to the toxicity of the current productivity narrative as well as the negativity of those who will have you believe that you must justify your yearning for an artistic life. The germ of this idea came from co-editor Gillian Turnbull, who on a cold day during the pandemic met with contributor Linda Browne to talk about writing. They stood on either side of a picnic table in a park near their housing co-op discussing how best to organize their time as external pressures came down on them to work more, harder, quicker. Suddenly the sacred space of home was gone, the lines between home life and work life blurred. Whereas once Gillian had carved out the time after coming home from work to write, she now couldn't justify logging off before bed. Nor, if she happened to find a moment to create, could she face yet more time onscreen.

Linda, still dealing with the effects that long Covid had had on her thinking and creative process, agreed. Add to this their domestic pressures—keep house, cook food, save money. Only someone with a partner who keeps home life going actually finds time to create, they joked. They both had artistic partners and shared responsibilities, and neither could understand how to implement the work model espoused by productivity experts like Cal Newport. There was no closing the office door to think, no segregating solo time for the purposes of creation. Someone needed to talk about this.

Before Gillian presented this idea to the collective, however, our fate had already been predicted. One slushy winter night in February 2019, our writing group—for that's what we were at the time—sat around a table in the party room at Christian's condo. We were pretty excited that night because Christian's mother, Geraldine Stringer, the famous psychic and subject of his memoir, would be joining us. Christian helped his mother into the room and got her settled in her chair. With an aura of authority that contradicted her frailty, she looked around the table and just began. No one was expecting a reading, but there we were, learning some surprising things from the woman who had spent a lifetime using her gifts to solve crimes, teach others how to tap into their own psychic abilities, and reassure her son that it was safe for him to fly.

Gillian was to win awards; Pamela was "the dark horse" and would surprise everyone, especially herself; Nellwyn had been torn on which program to attend, which was true; and then, most surprisingly, Geraldine told us that we would go into business together, or maybe work on a book together . . . none of us can remember her exact wording. We would often joke around about opening a writing retreat, mostly because we all really wanted a writing retreat, but how could a group of people write a book together? Whether the book you are holding is the fulfillment of a prophecy, evidence of the power of suggestion, or a complete coincidence, it is a poignant tribute to the late, great Geraldine Stringer, and the manifestation of collective creative power.

In this anthology, you will hear from Canadian and international writers from a breadth of backgrounds and experiences—many whom identify as BIPOC, women, LGBTQIA2S+, neurodivergent, and disabled. These writers represent a body of creators whose lives are not proscribed by predictable work schedules or reliable support systems; they fit creating into the cracks of their lives, those unexpected windows of time, and through their generous stories, show us all how to keep creating—not producing—in the face of systemic barriers and entrenched white patriarchy.

Like we said, we arrived at King's from different worlds and with different intentions.

For better or worse, Nellwyn has rarely experienced a distinction between art, work, and life. In her family of professional artists and art educators, drawing and singing and storytelling were bread and butter. As a child, it probably would have seemed strange to Nellwyn if her godfather *didn't* sing opera as they hiked their fly-fishing rods to the river. Making and teaching art professionally, full time, was not only possible but also demonstrably normal. Nellwyn was older than she would like to admit before she realized how anomalous this really is. It is painfully boring—not to mention obnoxious—to say that Nellwyn has always been a writer, but there is no other way to tell her story. She began in theatre, studying playwriting and devised theatre at York University before pursuing her MFA. Almost as soon as she landed at King's and met the people who would become her co-editors, Nellwyn knew she was exactly where she belonged. Since then, she has had the privilege of working with an incredible group of literary folks as an author, editor, bookseller, and teacher. It was community and collaboration that drew Nellwyn to theatre as an emerging artist, and *Bad Artist* is an opportunity to bring art, work, and life together again, in community.

For Pamela, the path to this anthology was more like a circuitous and often tedious detour, with no pretty towns to stop at or stunning vistas along the way to make it all worthwhile. A former copy writer turned newspaper copy editor turned corporate cog turned cook turned teacher of cooking turned teacher of writing, Pamela was looking for a way to make a living teaching—a vocation she realized in her fifth decade had been her calling all along. In conversation with the chair of the English department at Seneca College (now Polytechnic), she was told to get a master's degree and come back. And so, she did. But then she drank the MFA Kool-Aid and met people who inspired her, and she started writing a book (as was required by the program), caught up in the idea that maybe she could be a real writer instead ("real" meaning a published book author). Her book was, um, problematic, but Plan A panned out, and she has now taught at Seneca Polytechnic for nearly five years. But even better, she met this lot. For the other three editors, this is a chance for a second book, another credit, but for Pamela, it is an opportunity to insinuate herself into this wonderful group of talented writers and editors—like the dweeby kid on the schoolground getting invited to play with the cool kids.

Christian seemed destined for a writing career, yet embracing it took him nearly forty years. He hand-wrote his first book at age eleven while journeying with his famous mother across North America. The book, which foreshadowed his future interest in the sciences, depicted a doctor navigating the universe in a giant hospital spacecraft treating diverse alien species. Fast forward a few decades, and Christian's professional life became deeply entrenched in molecular cancer biology and basic science research, a dramatic departure from the realm of creative writing. That all changed during a book club meeting where Christian shared his unique upbringing with a celebrity psychic mother and his eagerness to write about his experiences. Gillian, who had just finished her own application to the King's MFA program, urged Christian to apply too. For Christian, the decision was easy. The chance to hone his writing skills and receive mentorship from published authors while maintaining his full-time job presented an opportunity too good to pass up. Yet, the most rewarding outcome from his time at King's was forming a writer's group—a quartet that continues to offer support and guidance.

Gillian was well into a dead-end career when she started writing. She taught music courses at Toronto Metropolitan University—courses that grew in number and capacity until she was collapsing under the weight of eight hundred students a year. No permanent position was forthcoming, and it was time to try something else. As her publication train paused, then stalled, she cast about for opportunities to write on the music she loved, landing a regular spot on the roots music site No Depression. It was here she found community and craved more; a place where she could write regularly and without the pretension of academia for a group of people who cared. Bit by bit, she published: short pieces, interviews, longer features, leading her to decide it was time to focus this energy into a book. At King's, she found Nellwyn and Pamela and realized early on these were her people. She wrote a few manuscripts, most of which suffocate in her virtual desk, and looked forward to the group's regular meetings.

When searching for a publisher for this collection, a common response that came with various rejections was that they couldn't see how four people could edit a book. Considering our disparate backgrounds, our disparate lives, it does seem improbable. And yet, with a seamlessness that sometimes surprises even us, we text, we work together in a shared document, we nudge and encourage and burnish this product of our collective desire to tell the world that art matters, whatever its form.

We hope that you enjoy, reflect, and hold fast to the shared conviction that each of these essays embodies: that the creative drive is essential in the truest definition of the word—for it is in our essence to create, to make and write beautiful things. Before there was commerce, before there was capitalism, before there was that thrum of judgment and exhortation to produce, there was art. Simple. Beautiful. Human.

I

I'm So Lazy, I Can't Stop Crying

June 21, 2021.

Monday.

"Am I lazy?"

I ask this of my *Some Lines a Day Five-Year Memory Book*. I've not really had any time off between January 2020 and June 16, 2021. Now, five days into this break between work contracts, I'm already challenging the slowness that settles over me.

The next day states: "This week I have sewn: a shirt, leggings, a table cover for my mom, pants; planted some ginger and cat grass." I also painted a wall on the seventeenth. After that, the journal entries pause until August 23.

With all this blank space, we can only presume I was, indeed, lazy.

What a bad word, *lazy*. Coming, etymologists assume, from the German *lasich*, or languid, idle, its modern primary use centres around intent: being unwilling to work. Showing a lack of effort or care. Slow, sluggish, indolent.

"What is a better word for lazy?" Google prompts. *Slothful*, it answers. I guess by *better*, Google means more evocative, not more positive.

Perhaps, says the internet, laziness is a lack of motivation or confidence. Google's search prompts are spiralling inward: "Are humans inherently lazy?" "Do lazy people's brains work harder? (i.e., keep going and we'll find the legitimate excuse for our laziness . . .)." "What does God say about laziness?" I decide to finally stop when I reach the page of Geneva College, on a post titled "The Soul of the Lazy Man Desires, and Has Nothing . . ." The proverb continues below: ". . . but the soul of the diligent shall be made rich."

Google Books Ngram Viewer reports that incidents of the word *lazy* are relatively consistent across published volumes between 1800 and 1980, at which point they skyrocket, peaking in 2019.

It was probably around 1983 when I first felt worthless. Though I'd argue my previous five years of existence weren't devoid of worthlessness, it's just that I don't remember them. I'm encased in, built by, worthlessness; its viscous matter chugs cyclically somewhere in my body between layers of nerves and skin.

I joined the world during a violent thunderstorm in the summer of 1978, presaging the Winter of Discontent. Did my arrival bring it about? Or did that winter shape me instead? All I've ever known is that I am a working body and I am devoid of value if I am not labouring.

While snowstorms raged and picket lines swelled in the UK, I dawdled, already something of a lazy late bloomer in my first few months of life, engaging in useless activities like snoozing, crying, and staring out the window. Mom swaddled my worthlessness in sundresses, onesies, then bonnets and baby blankets, cooing words to counter the rising internal inadequacy, not knowing I'd never, ever meet expectations. Overseas, organized labour rose, collapsed, fell; private unions led the charge then bore the responsibility when conservative governments punctured collective action. And thus into the workforce I was thrust, understanding I was only meant to shoulder my way through, on my own, every waking moment of my life.

.

Some Lines a Day contains mostly mundane recreations of my quotidian time: "I have a headache"; "I was overcharged for peaches"; "The cats want to go outside"; "I have a migraine"; "I lost my temper"; "We ate pizza and played crib. Boyfriend won." My only references to work are complaints: "Marking"; "Still marking"; "FUCK MY LIFE STILL MARKING."

"When will I ever write?" I ask *Some Lines a Day*, not infrequently.

It does not answer me.

It becomes the central gathering place for my writing attempts. I tease with anecdotes: funny how the boyfriend's birthday happens on the same date every year. I might write a book on the cyclical ripping off my local yellow grocery store engages in. The anecdotes don't travel beyond the narrow rectangle in which they're written.

I draw pictures. I am not an artist.

Some Lines a Day lingers on my desk, sometimes closed for months at a time, but often the singular recipient of my creative energy. It is the only place where I am not judged for not producing.

Over in the UK, The Police climbed the charts while I was climbing the stairs in our tiny, rented townhouse. By 1979, the group was coasting on the success of sophomore album *Reggatta de Blanc*, thwarting the high likelihood that Sting might have trod in his father's footsteps, being an industry man in post-war England. Instead of heading to the shipyard, Sting was stadium bound.

In "Bring On the Night," Sting laments the day that has gently passed him by. Yet another day. It is the quotidian manifest in song: The track never really picks up, or settles in. It passes by. The instruments hover over a tentative beat in the verses, Sting's voice threadbare and fragile. The chorus allows a slightly stronger reggae anchoring, but the band prefers to twirl around the twinkling guitar, tossing their words into the darkening sky.

Just another day.

Wasted.

The shipyard Sting's father worked in, in the town of Wallsend, was part of British Shipbuilders, a public corporation created in 1977 to nationalize the industry. By 1982, British Shipbuilders had closed half its operations, sending the rest of its shipyards into the embrace of privatization. Sting's father died of cancer in 1987, the same year his employer Swan Hunter was resorbed into the private realm.

In 1983, Sting announced he was leaving The Police. "Every Breath You Take" topped the charts. Its album, *Synchronicity*, went double platinum in the UK, gold in the US. As the band played Shea Stadium that year, Sting decided he was done. Peak success for The Police cleared a path for Sting to go his own way. Every man for himself.

I entered kindergarten in 1983, wearing my pink Big Bird sweatshirt on the first day.

Laziness was not an option. Fortified learning was the name of the elementary game for me; my recesses and lunches and regular classes were cushioned by a program of brain testing, sessions with the resource teacher, advanced curriculum that I surpassed in Grade 1, then Grade 3, then Grade 4. I never bothered with Grade 2. I felt pretty bad through all of that, the threat of failure darkening my otherwise sunny childhood. When I made it to Grade 4, I started telling people, "I can't do this." No one listened.

By then I'd internalized my self-reliance. Nobody was coming to help me. I had to make it, and make it fast. Homework being what it was in the mid-eighties, I filled the rest of my time with other activities: after school and nights a blur of piano lessons, dance lessons, half-chewed meals swallowed in haste, childhood migraines. I learned to work fast, if not well. I produced. *Here is a play I wrote, please attend my handbells concert, I would like to submit this article to the newspaper, why don't I attend the young writers' conference.*

Go

Go

Go

Most of the unions lost their power in the 1980s. Not just in the UK, whose government simply led the way in creating legislation that would defang unions around the world. Employers took advantage, scaring organizing workers into abandoning their efforts with the threat of closure, offshoring work, contractualizing formerly permanent jobs. My dad travelled for work sometimes, spent nights and weekends running us around. My mom worked into the late hours of the night. I piled on the extra-curriculars, started a part-time job in 1993 at fifteen.

Somehow, by sixteen, I was part of a union. That year was also the first time someone documented my laziness on paper.

"Gillian needs to pull up her socks," my supervisor noted on an evaluation form, the pink carbon copy of which still lives in my old files. "Gillian, I know you are capable of doing a better job."

She yelled at me in the grocery store office. I punched out and took the bus home. To be honest, I didn't really care about groceries.

At home, though, I kept producing.

"If I Ever Lose My Faith in You" kept playing on my radio.

I failed math. I mean, utterly failed. I was put in remedial school, as this blossoming new narrative had an unacceptable ending for my parents. I spent Saturday mornings with other failures, thinking about all I could be doing outside that classroom. Meanwhile, I had gained full employment as the foremost expert on worthlessness. My internal calendar filled with invitations to speak at length.

I watched the competition grocery store go on strike. I learned terms like scab, and what it meant to cross a picket line for fresh celery. My wage went up twenty-five cents an hour to compensate for our ballooning crowds. I prepared to audition for music school. I auditioned. I failed.

By that point, public sector jobs in Britain had fallen by twenty-nine percent.[1] Correspondingly, stable wages, union protection, permanent contracts, health benefits, and pensions were on the decline. Jamie Peck and Adam Tickell, in a paper on neoliberalism, called the economic conditions chronically unstable, contradictory, and crisis ridden.[2]

I got a second job.

Laziness is something of a social contract, no? It can only exist in relation to something—or someone—else. Laziness can't exist inherently in a person; it is only recognized, made visible, in response to the relative effort of another.

Feelings of worthlessness correspond with a high rate of both attempted and successful suicide. Multiple studies link worthlessness and guilt to such ideation.[3] The only way to get past it, says my dad, is to do something. Clean the bathtub, go for a walk, pick up a guitar. Get busy. Find purpose. Do not languish.

Lazy: to be languid, idle.

I stacked up my to-do list, fending off the demons.

My second union went on strike in 2008, a poorly timed attempt to curry public favour. I walked the picket lines, added up my strike hours, handed the tally to the union bosses so I could continue working on other things in the off time. "I'm busy," I claimed in emails, phone calls, texts. The economy collapsed further. I was proud of myself for my full calendar, my self-imposed pressure. Collections companies called, then harassed. I amassed what I now call the Failure File: a series of notices threatening to end my healthcare, ruin my credit rating, shut off my utilities. I joined a third union and learned it was better to ingratiate oneself to the boss instead of radicalize, so I offered myself up for more, and more, and more work. I stood in corners, unnoticed, and watched the louder, lazier people discover that unions only offer so much protection.

By the way, Swan Hunter, Sting's father's employer, closed down for good in 2007.

I've been hiding the truth. *Some Lines a Day* is primarily a record of nature. "Here is a squirrel who stores pizza crusts on my balcony," I write and draw a fuzzy picture of a brown squirrel. The tail's colours bleed through to the next page.

A blackbird lands on the balcony one March afternoon and entrances my two cats for the day. The cats, named Emily and Martie after country band The Chicks, are furious they can't kill him. We name the bird Toby Keith.

Toby Keith becomes a throughline in *Some Lines a Day*.

The leaves have changed.

The money tree is growing.

The buds are incredibly slow this year.

A freak snowstorm killed my basil seedlings.

Martie ate a cicada and frothed at the mouth.

I draw pictures of violent thunderstorms.

I don't tell anyone about my entries. They would find out I was staring out the window.

Otherwise, I do not write.

Boyfriend hears that Sting is coming to town with his musical *The Last Ship*. His buddy is the musical director so we are comped seats. We are in awe—a labour musical with Sting as the star? We hang around backstage, talk to his friend; Sting emerges tall, solid, and charismatic, steps his way past me. We talk all the way home about *how much art he has made*.

But Sting claims this was his only way out of an extended songwriter's block. The "pensive, musically omnivorous, proudly erudite songwriter . . . had 'lost my huge, burning desire to just put things on the page.'" What? He became concerned he was "washed up."[4] What?

I turn myself into a commodity, a walking list of accomplishments, future goals, prior achievements, lists of things to buy, make, work on, produce. By 2012, I'm working a couple of jobs; by 2016, it's up to five. Pride comes in the form of journal issues I edit: two, three, up to six a year. How many articles did I publish? My cv is now x pages long, my self-worth inches up with every new thing I "have" to do, every demand that keeps me from creating.

I start to get sick.

Meanwhile, I forsake pleasure, postponing watching the last season of *The Wire* until I can "enjoy it." Other pleasurable activities take on the dark sheen of work: if I don't learn to sew my way out of fast fashion, I am a bad citizen. Didn't complete this year's Goodreads Reading Challenge? Bad reader. I justify watching, listening, or reading by pairing it with a workout. I keep journal pages of books read and shows watched complete with a star system and length of time to completion. I am a robot, full of data, lacking in heart.

I send out proposals but my manuscripts become musty. I stop writing for pleasure.

The cancer arrives. I dream of small green monsters crawling into my neck and gnawing at my tissue, scrounging around for morsels. I keep producing. One more issue. One more essay graded. One more denial of opening my heart to November's falling yellow crunch, the brisk sniff of first snow, of putting these experiences into words on the page.

The anaesthetist puts me to sleep. I count backward for him, only making it to seven, thinking, *Thank god no one can ask me to do anything for a little while.*

When his memoir came out in 2003, Sting reflected on his father's death. "I think cancer is the result of undigested dreams and forcing yourself to do something that is not distinctively you."[5]

Is it possible that all this time the river has indeed been flowing? I wouldn't have dared tell anyone I noticed it for fear I'd be caught red handed: lazy; merely observing, not producing. But as Sting suggests, if I keep on this path, all that will be left of my crumbled empire of work is the stones discovered by the workmen. Where is my art? There is no point looking because it doesn't exist.

Wait. The river is still flowing, moving along to the sea. It is relentless. Like water, my words don't stop moving just because I put a container around them. They burst through, striking rivulets here and there. No one can see them but me.

Life continues. I wake up from the knife and I'm cured. One by one, I drop my jobs; by the end of 2017, I'm down to one. I write a book, it goes into the world. I write more. I stop. I start again. I stop.

Pressure mounts, the flow ebbs.

I don't notice that I've been tracking the moon, humming phrases of old country songs, watching the gradual drip of the faucet onto my toe in the bathtub. I don't catch the care with which I bake a loaf of bread or trim my tomato plants, the doodles on my notepad, the half-formed thoughts in margins of books. I forget that I spend the first half-hour of the morning staring at the leaves brushing my window, forming flickers of connection among the words I read the day before, the songs I heard. Rivulets, bursting through the seams of my container.

"If at any given moment, any decision you make is essentially determined by everything that has ever happened to you up to that point . . . this sense of you deciding to do something in the moment is just not true," says Steven Soderbergh in his discussion of *Determined: A Science of Life Without Free Will* by Robert M. Sapolsky. "No creative person wants to be told they didn't think of something."[6]

In September 2023, we go to see Sting in concert. The balm of the day doesn't lift after the sun sets; his voice drifts, tickling over the crowds to reach us, stirring us from the warm cocoon of air.

Has every day led to this point? The first songs are marked with a creak in his vocals, he is, before us, the culmination of his every experiment and failure and lost opportunity to this moment, as am I. Sting is gentle with his crowd; gratitude seeps around the corners of his inter-song banter. Why aren't I so gentle with myself?

I've been so focused on the product—words on the page—I didn't notice my creating was already spread all around me. I never stopped, I sublimated. It's always been there.

Sting ends the concert with "Fragile." Its hook is a circular, four-bar phrase, descending the neck of the guitar. Be careful, he warns in the lyrics, should we wreak violence upon ourselves and each other? Will the sun cry for us as we do?

Would I demand of others the level of productivity I violently impose on myself?

In the video for "Fragile," Sting shows us his effort. Partway through the guitar solo, he lifts his hand away, shakes out a cramp, wipes it on his leg. This art, it is not easy, he's saying. It is not the finished, polished product. He is in it, with it, part of it.

"Gillian seems distant and sometimes out of touch with her surroundings. Gillian shows little or no enthusiasm about her job. Gillian is very quiet and seems unapproachable."

Gillian is going to look out the window.

Gillian is going to observe for now.

Gillian made a list, but it blew away in the wind.

Gillian just might be lazy.

GILLIAN TURNBULL is the author of *Sonic Booms: Making Music in an Oil Town* (Eternal Cavalier Press, 2019). She holds a PhD in Ethnomusicology and an MFA in Creative Nonfiction. She has taught music at Toronto Metropolitan University and written for *Chatelaine*, *Maisonneuve*, *The Walrus*, and the *National Post*. She is the Director of Writing and Publishing at the University of King's College in Halifax.

In Defence of Giving Up

Three months after my daughter was born, I went to the launch of a friend's book at the Toronto Reference Library. It may sound ridiculous, but at the time it felt like a very brave thing to do. The event was one of my first postpartum outings alone, and certainly the first time I had seen many of my former publishing colleagues since I had disappeared into motherhood.

I had been looking forward to the launch for weeks, prepared myself mentally, pumped breast milk, planned an outfit, organized transportation, and relayed a feeding schedule. I was excited to be sans very new baby, excited to slip back into the life that was mine before her arrival upended it.

But as soon as I arrived, I felt uncomfortable. My new pants felt too snug over my slowly deflating belly, my nursing bra stuffed with breast pads out of a fear of leaks. After weeks and weeks of wearing something in the proximity of pyjamas (or "ma-jamas," as a writer friend had hilariously called them), the spectacular feat of getting dressed now weighed heavy with metaphor; I felt like I was putting on an outfit that didn't really fit, one that maybe wasn't right for me anymore but that I was clinging to regardless.

Going to a book launch was something I had done dozens if not hundreds of times before, and yet I felt glaringly out of place. I didn't know how—and maybe didn't even want—to make literary small talk; didn't know how to talk about anything at all other than my daughter, didn't remember how to be a person out in the world.

There were my friends from the newspaper I freelanced for; my friends from the magazine I worked at; my friends from the writing community at large. I should have been overjoyed to be near them after being cooped up in a single room with a screaming, sleepless infant for the better part of three months. But, in my ill-fitting clothes, I was totally consumed by the tiny world I'd left behind at home.

The beautiful, successful crowd gathered and took their seats, and instead I opted to lean against a concrete pole at the back of the room, a self-determined outsider accommodating the very real possibility of retreat. I checked the time and considered another glass of wine to make me more comfortable, taking mental inventory of that pumped milk at home in the fridge.

I loved my friend. Of course I wanted to support her and her wonderful new book. This was the kind of environment I had long felt at home in. I was supposed to want to be the person I was before—but all I really wanted to do was go home.

Before my daughter was born, in early 2018, I was mostly convinced my worth lay in writing eight hundred–word pieces in very little time for very little money. As a "permalancer," as we're now known, I earned my living and reputation by writing frequent, short pieces about timely issues for a consistent handful of publications, delivering each on a tight deadline and then measuring my credibility via clicks, likes, and shares.

At the time, I was also pretty sure that the price of that worth was having complete strangers call me all sorts of vile names on the internet, and that the insults and threats I commonly found in my inbox were part of what it meant to be "successful." Declining work wasn't part of the deal, but professional exhaustion, being treated badly, hustling and fighting to be heard for very little money on very little sleep definitely was.

As far as I was concerned, suffering gracefully was what it meant to be a professional writer, and turning things down—or even creating some reasonable boundaries—meant you just couldn't hack it. Besides, saying "no thanks" to invitations and assignments just meant that they would be handed to someone else standing right behind you, eager to take your place.

Better to be grateful, teeth gritted, with a smile on your face.

It's no exaggeration to say that we exist in a poisonously positive culture, one that constantly discourages us from complaining, calling things out, and, of course, quitting entirely. "Never give up," the personal mantras espouse; "Anything is possible," the Instagram squares scream—even when we're on the floor, unsure if we can self-care ourselves back up again.

"Living your dreams and pursuing your 'passion' isn't as easy as the motivational Pinterest quotes would have you believe," a 2018 Forbes article on the trend of permalancing asserts. "This is because companies can hire permalancers without making any real commitments to them. They can end contracts as they please, deny work if they want, and more significantly than anything else, there's no requirement to be offered a traditional benefits package, such [as] paid time off or health insurance."[1]

I have often stayed in situations—both personal and professional—that have actively harmed me, all the while clutching tight to those oft-repeated and pretty convincing "pursuing my passion" positivity messages. *If only I worked hard enough*, I would think. If only I gave it my all, put in those extra hours, exerted myself to the point of exhaustion. If only I was really, truly committed, burning myself out in pursuit of my lifelong dreams, then I could have everything I always wanted. Then people would respect me. Then I would be successful.

Because of that particularly insidious "never quit" belief

system—one that so many of us adhere to—I have stayed with people who have harmed me, under bosses who have demoralized me, in living and working situations where I was floundering. When it comes to writing, I have produced work on impossibly unaccommodating deadlines, for incredibly bad pay, for some not so nice people; pieces that garnered online abuse with little or no support from the publications I wrote them for, that paid in exposure or in (exact quote) "a little extra money I should be grateful for."

In that spirit of "I can do it," I have put off rest, and care, and healing. I have tried to prove myself worthy by what I can take, by how much I can suffer, by how far I will go—certainly not by how well I write, and definitely not by how well I can take care of myself.

And, by doing all this, I have learned a pretty nasty truth; the more you endure, the more you will be asked to endure.

It's a well-worn cliché to say that a baby changes you. Some would even say it's a smug sentiment, spoken by people justifying the fact that their lives have been irrevocably altered, and not necessarily for the better. But I don't actually think it's necessary to have a baby to see the necessity of slowing down, of asserting boundaries, of saying a loud "no, thank you" instead of yes to every opportunity—it just happened to be necessary for me.

My personal process of "giving up" began almost ten years ago now, slowly and carefully and with great resistance. The first step came when I quit the security of that full-time magazine job, a job that I loved, that long defined me (and my social life), that gave me worth and access to the world I was craving. It was also very obviously a job that was making me unwell with overwork, something I both knew and denied. After finally facing the reality that what I was doing—and enduring—was unsustainable, I retreated into full-time freelancing, which in some ways was like replacing one kind of illness for another.

Given the particular way I have long been taught to approach work, freelancing just made me further incapable of rest with a bonus fear of scarcity. By the time my nonfiction collection came out in the spring of 2017, the frantic speed at which I had been working—pitching, filing, invoicing, repeat—was destroying me. The late nights, the early mornings, the answering work emails on vacation, the acceptance of abuse from social media as part of the job, the terrible work and health habits, the unrelenting stress and anxiety. I knew I had to start saying no. I had to start giving things up.

I can't entirely credit myself for making the move to embrace a slower pace—this, of course, is where the baby comes in. Getting pregnant a month after that book's launch was the invitation necessary for a genuine breather. Enduring vicious morning sickness during book-tour travel and book-related television and radio appearances gave me the perfect excuse to pare things down, to pull away from my unhealthy addiction to work, and I gladly took it.

Professional writing and publishing culture is packed with the kinds of jobs that people respect you for but don't pay overtime, or even that well at all. You may be admired by peers for your "glamorous" bylines, you may "matter" enough to be part of that beautiful, successful crowd, but you are also constantly on the verge of a health crisis, or an economic crisis, or a total breakdown.

That's the thing about the pervasive culture of overwork in publishing—it does everything in its power to make you stay stuck. It builds a mystique around what you do and who that makes you, so much so that you desperately miss the frenzy when it's gone, regardless of how much happier and healthier you are in its absence.

Despite the fact that I had long recognized the need to step away from the toxic speed of modern life, fundamental questions always lingered to prevent me from taking the leap: How do you find the balance between doing the work you love and care about in a way that is sustainable and healthy, while also finding a way to exist financially? Is that even possible? How do you define success? And where does your identity come from if not from your work?

I'll readily admit it's all well and good to say that we should all stop working at this widespread frantic pace, but for many that pace is what is necessary not only to stay relevant, but to survive. The fear that comes with logging off, tuning out, and turning things down is very real.

What's worse, an ability to tolerate general mistreatment now seems to be a desired contemporary working trait. Often when I got brave enough to ask where my cheque was, or for a reasonable amount of time or money to do a job, or even to not be so exposed to online trolls, I could almost hear the eyes rolling, my name crossed off a list of future options. I remember one publisher in particular just went ahead and wished me luck when I asked for a rate similar to what his male columnists were being paid. Another never emailed me again after I turned down a single job because of work overload (this after writing upward of fifty times for the publication). Still another stopped getting in touch when I said my new baby made the current assignment difficult (as if babies don't eventually grow up).

All of this weighed on me, of course, but after some time spent being forced to slow down (my daughter turned six this year), I'm certainly no longer convinced that teetering on the edge of burn-out is what success really looks like. I no longer think the only way to matter is by checking your email in the middle of the night, by over-scheduling and under-sleeping, by exposing yourself to abuse or destroying yourself in the process of "succeeding." Instead, I'm committed to trying to find genuine ways to resist the delirious pressure to always be producing.

While I was leaning on the concrete pole at that book launch, a former colleague of mine—someone I hadn't seen for many years—snuck over to say a quick hello. It was only a few moments before the onstage interview was to officially begin, so we caught up quickly in hushed tones, happily sharing general life updates.

She'd been an editor at the magazine that I myself had once worked at. She'd gone on mat leave and simply never come back. I admit there had been moments where I wondered what had happened to her, wondered why she'd given up such an "important" job and lifestyle. Now a mother of two, she was working on what I, at the time, deemed less high-profile projects.

She warmly congratulated me on my own new addition and asked me how it was going. I gave the usual appropriate, canned spiel that boiled down to "hard but good," and then, in my big-event-related vulnerability, confided how outside of everything I felt in that moment. How insignificant and boring and inconsequential my life was now compared to all these active, attractive media people. How small I felt because I was currently spending my days in ma-jamas instead of pitching and writing and filing and publishing (repeat).

She paused for a moment, so many more years into motherhood and much wiser than I, and smiled knowingly. "Well, maybe a small life can be a good life," she said.

Yes, we live in a culture that urges us to never quit, that tells us we must follow our dreams at all costs, that anything is possible. But one thing this toxic hustle culture doesn't teach us is just how healing it can be to simply surrender, give up, and let go. It doesn't tell us how and when to release our grip or guide us to a place of acceptance and openness to what we can become after doing so. It doesn't let on how liberating and powerful it can be to opt out and step away.

As much as I long subscribed to the false ethos of possibility that was all around me, as much as I worshipped at the altar of doing my best at all costs, I eventually learned the hard way that "anything" was not actually possible, no matter how many times it was printed in a girl boss book or on a novelty mug. I mean, it turns out I really shouldn't record an audiobook in-studio two weeks postpartum while wearing an adult diaper, or fly to cover a story with third-degree vaginal tearing, or make it to the press box for 7:00 PM while also being the sole food source for a newborn.

I know these are extreme examples, but each taught me a lot about the fallacy of the well-meaning phrase "we can make this work." It may feel like the right thing to say or think, but it can often be a bold-faced lie, and the more people who perpetuate that deception, the more damaging it becomes.

Sometimes you really just can't and shouldn't and instead have to give up and walk away. And however difficult, however much you feel like a failure as a result, it can often be really healthy and in your best interest to do so.

I think about standing at the back of that room at that book launch years ago, wondering if, by giving some things up, by saying no, and by letting go, I have succeeded in creating a Good, Small Life. What I do know is, at the very least, I have a better one—one where I have room to breathe, where I value my own worth over perceived prestige, where I don't care so much about joining the beautiful, successful crowd in their seats. I didn't quit writing, of course, only the parts of it that were harming me—and there's got to be some good in that.

Before I became pregnant with my daughter, I was at full sprint every day of the week, neglecting my body, my mental health, my self-preservation, my true sense of self. It took time to properly grieve my old life and identity, but I have since found room to breathe, think, and grow in ways I never would have thought possible.

There is great power in the self-compassionate process of consciously giving up. Yes, loosening my grip brought uncertainty and even disappointment, but it also (eventually) brought happiness; I no longer live in a cloud of buzzing worry, no longer feel a perpetual sense of failure, no longer bury feelings under a pile of poorly paid assignments. In many ways, I am starting all over again; I can't go back to that person who had destructive ambitions, was terrible with boundaries, who defined herself solely by her work, who surrendered her worth to arbitrary assessments and stranger's judgments.

I'm sure some people will read this and assume I am justifying what has been "taken" from me by becoming a mother, or even by just becoming too tired to go on, and that's fine. I would be lying if I didn't say I have moments where I miss aspects of my old life. But I also believe there will be people who will read this and recognize their own experience, who will understand there is a beauty in letting go of the very things we've been conditioned our whole lives to think, feel, and want.

Throughout our lives we all play a lot of roles, some prescribed and some adopted, some of them fitting better and feeling more authentic than others. Some are new and some are old, and some are somehow both. And sometimes we hold on tight to those that hurt us, just for the sake of holding onto them, not really sure why we're doing it at all.

What I've learned is this: If something doesn't value you, quit it. If something is actively harming you, quit it. If you genuinely hate something, quit it. Because despite what you've been told, despite what you've clung to and what people will say, giving up can actually be a very good thing.

STACEY MAY FOWLES is an award-winning journalist, critic, author of five books, and editor of four anthologies. Her bylines include *Reader's Digest, Elle Canada, Toronto Life, The Walrus, BuzzFeed, Vice, Hazlitt, Quill & Quire, The Athletic,* and others. Her national bestseller, *Baseball Life Advice*, was released in spring 2017, and was selected by the *Globe and Mail*, the *National Post*, and *Maisonneuve* as a best book of the year. A former columnist at the *Globe and Mail*, she released her first children's book, *The Invitation*, in spring 2023.

Learning to Love the Fallow Periods

A field can lay fallow for one to five years depending
on the crop.

—Darcy Larum, "What is Fallow Ground: Are There
Any Benefits of Fallowing Soil"

"Are you going to plant a garden this year?" my friend asked.
He sips his G&T. Honeybees buzz from blossom to bloom
through his garden. Bright green shoots and buds appear on
stems and in the soil. The promise of hot summer nights is in the
spring breeze.

My chest swells, tightens. I try to think of an eloquent way to
say, "I can't. Not this year." I try to think of explanations or excuses that will ease my guilt. There will be no bright red tomatoes or
curving cucumbers. Not this year.

I can't do it all. I can't have it all, I think. I start to explain that
with my Master of Fine Arts starting that summer, I just don't
think I'll have time for school and my full-time job, all the other
things that come with being a human, and tending to a garden. I
say it like I'm apologizing. (But to whom?)

"It's just a fallow period," he says. "Gardens need fallow periods."

He says it with the wisdom I love from him. At the time, I didn't
recognize that maybe he saw something beyond the conversation

we were having; because now, three years after that warm evening on his deck, ice cubes jingling against glass, my garden is still fallow, and last year, my writing went fallow. I didn't call it that, not then. Instead of a fallow period, I (and others) have named it: a lull, wintering, writer's block, a break, self-care, refuelling, regenerating, recharging, quitting, failure, loss. The word I use to describe it depends on my state of mind, and while I don't always see the value, it's necessary.

> Any farmer will tell you, the most time-consuming work is cultivating the soil. The harvest is the last part. And yet, we are taught to rush to this last part. To believe that something should grow merely because we command it to. This is nothing short of a magic trick . . . There is no writer's block (IMO). But only a lack of soil.
> —Ocean Vuong

Overwhelm is the stage before fallow. I don't enter a fallow period knowing it's what my body, creative mind, mental health need. I fall face first into it. I collapse into a state of dis-ease where I can't. I can't think of words. I can't form sentences. I can't place commas, periods, quotation marks. I question where a paragraph should start or finish. I can't connect thoughts. I can't stand confidently behind my ideas. I can't trust myself to create because after over-whelm and the fallow period that follows is the clichéd existential crisis. I'm not good enough. My words are not enough. I will never be like [insert artist/writer I admire]. The pull to self-loathing and dread is strong.

The early stages of a fallow period can include:

- Binge-watching *Shetland* while drinking endless cups of tea, coffee, hot chocolate. I watch the BBC crime drama even though I've watched every episode at least five times, but the familiarity is soothing. The accents a warm bath. I shop for knit jumpers online. (I use "jumper" now because I feel like I should live on a croft on the Shetland Islands.)

- Finding the perfect vegan brownie recipe and making it over and over again until my teeth ache and my body starts to reject the taste of chocolate and walnuts. But never sugar.
- Walking in the rain along soggy forest trails. I find a favourite trail. Its familiarity, like *Shetland*, is comforting and necessary. The landscape shifts and changes with the seasons. Boughs stretch and shrink. Leaves unfurl and brown. This place is inside me and it holds me somehow.
- Taking pictures of every meal I cook, eat. I also consider photographing the ingredients as they are cooked, cut, and prepared. I share these on Instagram and Twitter/X, because at least I'm cooking, at least I can make food and feed myself. That counts for something, right?

> I have come to realize that a lull is not just an occupational problem. It is an emotional, intellectual, and existential one as well. If I ever find an answer, I figure I will feel less fatalistic about intervals, periods of unemployment or dormancy, fallow times. I might be easier on myself and engage in less-anxious behaviour.
> —Kyo Maclear, *Birds Art Life: A Year of Observation*

The days, weeks, months before a fallow period feel like the stages of grief and like grief, it's not a ladder I climb one rung at a time, upward, until I'm at acceptance and hope. After a few good, productive days, I wake up the same way I always do, perform the ritual of making coffee, checking Twitter/X, and sit down to find out I've slid back down the ladder a few rungs. I sit unable to think of a single word to type, my mind blank.

Writing is hard. It's not endless streams of perfect prose and evocative scenes. The muse doesn't always come when I call her, she doesn't even come when I beg and plead and barter. Sometimes the words feel like pulling long slivers from the tender flesh where my fingernails and fingers meet. Questioning why I chose this life dominates all waking hours. These ruminations become desperate and irrational. I don't sleep. I download meditation apps and ASMR tracks, learn box breathing to ease the anxiety and panic.

Is it worth it? I think as my heartbeat slows and my inhales and exhales return to my body.

I've lain my face on my desk and cried. The wood warm from my palms and forearms that stretch toward my expectant, almost taunting keyboard. I want to wrench my whole body, mind, and spirit away from my desk and computer. I want to bake cookies, to walk down the hill to the brewery and drink cold beer with a friend. I want to watch hours and hours of Anthony Bourdain on *Parts Unknown.* I don't want to write. I don't want to read. I don't want to think about writing or reading.

Then fear sets in. If I wander away, if I rip myself from my craft, will it turn its back on me? Will it be there when I'm ready to come back?

> Wintering is a season in the cold. It is a fallow period in life when you're cut off from the world, feeling rejected, sidelined, blocked from progress, or cast into the role of an outsider . . . Some winterings creep upon us more slowly, accompanying the protracted death of a relationship, the gradual ratcheting up of caring responsibilities as our parents age, the drip-drip-drip of lost confidence . . . However it arrives, wintering is usually involuntary, lonely, and deeply painful. —Katherine May, *Wintering: The Power of Rest and Retreat in Difficult Times*

My last fallow period spread over four months. In its early days, I refused to give in. If I kept writing, if I showed up at my desk, I'd push through and the words would come. I would create by force. Instead of waiting for the muse or inspiration, I would make it happen.

Sentences were written. A handful of words connected by an undercurrent of duress. When I read them now, they are empty, strangled and bound. The act of writing during those early days was exhausting. My body ached and hung heavy. It was reacting to the fatigue that sat in my soul and ate at my creative spirit. For months, through my MFA, I wrung out every drop of creative juice I had, and as I sat down in the months that followed, with my new degree hanging on the wall, I braced myself for the reality that I may not have what it takes to be a writer. For a decade I wrote as a journalist and thought that with a creative writing degree I'd be able to call myself a writer. Instead, a new bar was set, and every time I sat down to write I battled my insecurities.

When writers talk about craft, they refer to the practice and commitment of learning a skill that evolves and grows over time. It's akin to carpentry or ceramics. Hours of time and focus are expected to be a "good" writer. For me, writing craft involves another kind of craft, not the kind that includes scissors and white glue, but witchcraft. I both fear and am deeply fascinated with witches. There's something terrifying and awe-inspiring about their power, and because of this I've brought a bit of the occult into my writing practice. Many writers do, even if they don't call it that. We're superstitious people, we have patterns and rituals connected to our work. There are morning people and evening people. There are writers with a special writing sweater. There are writers who drink wine, drink coffee, drink bourbon while writing. Some need music—pop songs from their youth, instrumental jazz—while others can only create in silence with ear plugs in. I have an element of all these things woven into my practice, but sometimes I think if I knew how to cast a protection spell over myself and my writing, I would. I want to protect myself from the fear and self-doubt that plagues writers and creative people everywhere. What keeps me from googling "protection spells" is the scene from the middle of *The Craft* when Nancy becomes "too" powerful and greedy and is struck by lightning after doing the "Invocation of the Spirit." Instead, I light banishment candles infused with sage, I draw tarot cards and roll ritual oil on my wrists.

Rituals and habits are as much a part of witchcraft and writing as they are of farming and gardening. As a gardener, before the dirt became overrun with blackberry brambles and morning glory, I wandered the beds thick with tomato vines and raspberry canes. I inhaled the fresh, pungent smell of the leaves, I dived my fingers into the dark soil. I looked for blight and leaf curl. I read books about companion gardening. I watered in the evening and used a kelp fertilizer every three weeks. I did quiet incantations for rain.

Even when a crop is fallow, work is happening elsewhere or even below the surface. We don't see the worms and insects burrowing and adding nutrients to the soil. We don't see the farmer or gardener whose attention is turned to different tasks and other crops that need their care.

Sometimes when I'm sitting still, seemingly idle in a car or a park during the weekday, I find myself tuning into a certain kind of talk. What are these people even doing here, someone will say with a scolding air. Don't they have jobs? In these moments, I resist the urge to defend myself. I fight the rising tide of indignity and cultivate patience, the hardest crop of all. Just wait, I think. Someday, you might just read the fruits of my invisible labour. —Bonnie Tsui, *You Are Doing Something Important When You Aren't Doing Anything*

If economists sat down and evaluated my energy input versus my successful output, they'd have questions about my productivity. It's here where many of us creatives get stuck. We want to be successful and the definition of success, which is framed by capitalism and productivity, doesn't align with creativity.

From the outside, those who don't know a creative life look out at the bare soil of an artist's fallow period and see a failed crop, a forgotten landscape. The word barren might come to mind. I heard early on in a lecture, or maybe I read it in one of those craft essays that are passed around between writers, that most of our writing happens away from our desk and computer. I've repeated this line to students, to other writers, but it's been hard for me to accept this as true. If no one can see the way my brain is dealing with the structure problem in the fifth chapter while I'm washing my hair, does it count as work? When many of us think of work, we still think of black-and-white footage of people (men) in coveralls, maybe floppy hats with stout warped brims tipped over their dark eyes, working along a conveyor belt in a Ford factory.

Our ideas of work bring to mind industrialization, machinery, mass production for mass efficiency. I know writers who have systems. They outline and use index cards and schedules and self-imposed deadlines. They churn out work and their names appear in the bylines of the journals and magazines dropped in my mailbox. I immediately think "these writers are successful," but we don't see the invisible labour. As a woman, I should be familiar with the unseen work done. The small things, little tasks, big problems solved by women while no one is watching or paying attention. I know as writers it's hard to talk about our fallow periods (we're getting better at it). It's hard to say, "I'm not writing because I can't" because when I think those words, the next thoughts are, *Maybe I'm not a writer. Maybe now they all see me for the fraud I am.*

When I've leaned into my fallow periods and stopped resisting the lulls in my creativity, I give myself time to be the person and the writer I need to be without the pressure of productivity and output hanging over me. The pressure is still there, like the late August mosquito that hovers waiting for the moment when you're not paying attention. But as I move through overwhelm and fear toward fallow, another part of me wakes up. A part that has been quietly absorbing all the tips and quotes about self-care that I scroll past as I make coffee or soak in the bath. A part that no longer rolls her eyes at suggestions to take a break, to take time for myself. It's not loud, but it starts saying, *Maybe this isn't working. Maybe sleeping in, and putting the work aside is what you need?*

I stop setting the alarm for 6:00 AM. I sleep until 7:00 (because that's sleeping in now). I don't open new Word documents with the intention of writing an essay about my love for '90s teen heartthrobs. I don't revise and edit. I make cookies and binge watch three seasons of *Virgin River*. I read fiction and poetry and books entirely unrelated to my work-in-progress. I go camping and leave pens and paper on my desk. I fight the urge to be productive, I fight the guilt that claws at me, knowing this isn't forever, but it's what's needed now.

As a journalist **MEGAN COLE** has worked for community newspapers, CBC Radio, and Canadian Press. Her creative nonfiction has appeared in *The Ex-Puritan, Invisiblog, untethered, Hungry Zine, Chatelaine,* and *The Fiddlehead.* Megan is immersed in '90s pop culture including endlessly listening to the Backstreet Boys as she works on her first creative nonfiction book. When Megan isn't writing, reading, knitting, or cooking, she's working as the director of programming and communications for the BC and Yukon Book Prizes. She lives and works on the territory of the Tla'amin Nation in BC.

Getting Off the Couch

Greetings and salutations. Come, have a seat, and let's have a good ole catch-up. I believe that the power of the words shared among friends can divide grief and multiply joy. Bring it all; there isn't much I haven't heard that will scare me away (pinkie promise).

Because, let me guess, if you're like most people, you've got some stuff that's working great and some things that could use some improvement. I do, too. It's part of life. I'd be willing to bet it's the struggles that bring you to these pages. We've all faced hardships at times and might not know what to do. You stew over these issues, complain, or vent about them. Maybe you're more like me: stuck on the couch so deep in a rut, suffering from writer's block or some other creative constipation, and you're not sure if there's anything you can do about it anymore.

Hey, I get it; change can be scary and hard. Some of us relish change while others shudder, dragging their feet every step of the way. I find myself somewhere in the middle, as summed up on the side of a flask: "I'll get over it; I just need to be dramatic first." (When I found that bottle in a shop, I'd never felt so seen.) After my moment of freak out or crankiness, I can get over myself and then adapt as necessary.

Let me ask you this: If you had the power to improve one thing in your life, what would it be? Where are you showing up in your own life, and where are you not?

I'll give you the same common-sense process I use to get over my bullshit and off the couch. When I put this into practice, it worked and brought me back to creating. Simple, yes; easy, no. Worth it? Surely. (Yes, I'm taking my advice, and I promise I won't ask you to do anything I haven't done.)

It all started with my nose . . .

My mother will tell you my nose is my best feature. It is straight, called "cute as a button," and holds my glasses in place, allowing me to see. However, looks can be deceiving. As it turned out, I had a severely deviated septum, causing breathing, snoring, and congestion problems. Despite people telling me time and time again that there must be a problem because no one sounds like they're snoring when they're awake, I denied it and resisted going to the doctor. It was only when I made a voice memo and heard breathing sounds drowning out what I wanted to hear that I finally went to the doctor, got some tests done, received a diagnosis, consented to surgery, and scheduled a date.

After successful surgery, the doctor summed it up as such: I hadn't been breathing out of either side of my nose for a long time. Welp. Now, there was hope for less congestion and better, deeper, and quieter breath. Post-surgery, after an extensive visual examination, Mom was happy to see that my nose looked the same. My breathing and quality of life are so much better with an internally realigned nose. I breathe better, I'm less congested, and the dog's happy because I stopped snoring.

The doctor ordered rest while recuperating from surgery, and I did most of that on the couch. When I first sank onto the cushions, it was great. No one was looking for me, and all I had to do was recover and heal. However, it got to the point where there was only so much streaming content, home renovation shows, and procedural drama reruns I could handle before I had to do something else. I couldn't concentrate on much yet for long, and indeed, certainly, nothing demanding any creative thought. So, I banged out a few jigsaw puzzles in as many days, ordering more for next-day delivery to keep up with the sudden demand.

It was great for a while, until it wasn't. I found myself stuck on the couch, as though the leather itself sucked me in, keeping me from re-engaging with life. Medically, the doctors cleared me to resume life as I knew it. I could move my head again, bend over, and brush my teeth with my mouth closed. Except I wasn't there mentally. So, on the couch, I stayed. Yes, I still did the bare minimum of what others expected of me, showing up for work, meetings, and appointments as they appeared on my calendar. I lost the impetus to write, make, and create to the couch: all the things that bring me to life. I knew nothing was going to change unless I did something different.

Change happens when you reach the point when you've had enough of your nonsense, don't want to talk about the same thing day in and day out anymore, and cannot stand living in the same mental or metaphorical place for one more minute. Our life serves and rewards us until it doesn't. And the couch was winning; the more I languished on the furniture, the less I showed up for myself. As each day passed where nothing got done, tomorrow was the magical place and time where something was going to change, and I would get something, some writing done, maybe? Crack open the journal?

I found myself stuck in the quicksand of the Saturday morning cartoons of my youth, rapidly sinking with diminishing hope of escape. Instead of sand, I found myself sinking into a quagmire of fears and doubts. Except, there was still enough time for rescue. Instead of waiting for the superhero, I would have to rescue myself. For a long time, I wanted to write. I had ideas, aspirations, and musings cultivated over the years, and I talked about them all the time. However, when it came time to put pen to paper or fingers to keys, I froze. I procrastinated, delaying creating by taking in other people's creative efforts, reading, scrolling, or watching. These fears and doubts turned me into the poster child for proving Newton's First Law of Motion, where a body (or a mind) will stay at rest unless or until an external force acts upon it.

It was then I realized something: We're all aligned to something. My nose looked good, even when it was still internally misaligned. To the outside world, I looked like I had it all pulled together and was doing well by society's standards: I had friends, family, a good home, a job, and a great dog. On the inside, it was a different story: I found myself conflicted about what, if anything, I wanted to do creatively and plagued by the fears of success and failure. Like my nose, things that look good outside don't always reflect what's happening internally. It's incumbent upon each one of us to decide where we want to go, what we achieve, and who we become. We are the summation of all our past experiences and lessons. The beauty is that we can pause to take stock of where we are, compare that to where we want to go next, and head in a new direction.

I noticed this with my nose. I had a problem breathing; small boys would find the amount of nasal mucosal excess in my nose utterly fascinating. My normal daytime breathing sounded like someone's nocturnal snores. I went to the doctor, she examined me, and we came up with a plan. Pausing to take stock makes it possible to work on the problems you can and want to solve. Spoiler alert, humans are hardwired to solve problems. Why not solve the ones that will get me closer to where I want to go and who I want to be?

More and more, I realized how far off I was from fulfilling my needs, wants, and desires—from my purpose. I would become a permanent part of the furniture if I didn't do something soon. Fundamentally, I didn't like the person I was becoming. To realign and course correct, I started to take some stock, taking a snapshot of where I sat. I started looking at what was working for me, what I was grateful for, and the resources I could leverage. For giggles, I also jotted down the list that's easier to come up with: what are the things that need to be improved? Because our brains can be assholes, this list is always easier to cultivate because it's right there in your face all the time. In some ways, it's easier to believe the naysayers, the ones who don't believe in us and squash our creative dreams. The danger comes when those external voices become the inner monologue. If not, the judgmental people in our lives are always more than willing to remind us. It's the stuff that keeps us up at night.

To keep the list a bit more manageable, I split it once more:

- What was in my control to modify
- What didn't belong to me
- What I could and could not influence

I realized there's an (imperfect) split between the internal and external.

The following page contains a short example of what I've come to call the Taking Stock Grid.

I can use the skills, aptitudes, and lessons honed over time to help me now. Listing them out gave me a concrete reminder of past progress and successes. The things working outside my control are what I called Life's Boons: public goods I get to use and enjoy. I give them a kiss of gratitude as I go about my day and do not take them for granted. Lastly, the things outside my control are those that don't belong to me. Letting go of that stuff is something I struggled with tremendously. And then I noticed the Astroturf.

As I sat outside, I heard the sprinklers turn themselves on. Looking up, I realized they were watering a piece of Astroturf. At first, I didn't know if there was a point in watering the plastic grass. According to my gardening friends, there isn't one. Then I understood that worrying about the things beyond your immediate power is as effective or beneficial as watering some Astroturf. Yes, you

Taking Stock Grid

	Within My Control	Outside My Immediate Influence
What's Working	Skills: writing, editing, creating, idea generation, strategy Health: hydration, meditation, breath, sleep, mindset, gratitude Connection: cultivating relationships Belongings cleaned out, well maintained	Art, music, books, libraries, and museums Friends and family's kindnesses, generosity, health, and cooking Community support and networks Nature, expanded walking trails Wi-Fi, power, and indoor plumbing
What Needs Improvement	Doctor's orders: more cardio and exercise. Get off the couch, fewer carbs/more vegetables More art, creativity, and writing Not showing up for myself and taking care of everyone else. Mindset Professional satisfaction, idea implementation, and execution Improving my corner of the world—take a stand, volunteer, contribute	Letting Go: Dealing with other people's bad news, poor behaviour, and what people think of me Problems that aren't mine Old limiting thoughts and beliefs that no longer serve me Daily weather The general state of the world

can do it. There aren't any good reasons *to* do it. Over time, watering it and worrying become a waste of water and mental energy. When fake grass gets watered every afternoon at 4:00, the ground still gets saturated. Where wet Astroturf covers ground, weeds still grow through the artificial grass. Whatever you feed and water sprouts. It's a metaphor as old as dirt itself (no, I'm not sure if I intended that pun or not). The more attention I pay to the things outside my control, the more energy I expend on what I can't influence, leaving less mental energy for the things I can impact.

Here's a small example: Since making this discovery by the pool deck, I've started checking in with myself to see if I'm watering the Astroturf or not. When something happens, I ask what I can do to move the situation forward. A friend called recently, telling me she's received some bad news from the doctor. She was upset, as was I. Once we got off the phone, I felt and processed what I needed to feel. I then did something different—I asked myself, "Am I watering the Astroturf? If so, then what was my part to play in this situation?"

I couldn't take on her pain, shock, or severity of the diagnosis. I couldn't wrap her in a bubble either because she's too independent to let me, and it's not that feasible anyway. However, I could do something; I could walk alongside her through these challenges, letting her take the lead. I could listen, drive her to the doctor, and pick up takeout. I found peace at that moment, identifying my role, and letting the pieces outside my capabilities go.

I noticed something else that proved helpful. I immediately noticed I had more mental capacity when I folded the grid in half, thereby letting go of the right half of the list. I felt more peace and less stress, which allowed me to respond to what was mine with more grace, calm, and creativity.

It was time to start looking at the remaining half of the grid. What was one thing I could start to get me off the couch and re-enter the world? Looking at the bottom left list, I started at the top and decided it was high time to stand up and put one foot in front of another.

It was one of the first great days of spring in New England, the kind of days that almost make up for the winters and rainy sloppy mess that brings in early spring. And the sunshine beckoned me outside.

I heeded the call. The name of the game was to get off the couch, get the legs moving for a bit, and check out how the work on the expanded walking paths was coming along. So, in the athleisure I'd been wearing for the past year, I tied up my running shoes, put earbuds in, and set off. I took off without considering time, distance, or pace.

Now, most of the time, habit, time management, or productivity management gurus would say that I needed to have goals in mind, broken down into appropriate steps, with deadlines, preparing myself to root any lofty ambitions. I wasn't there yet. I wasn't ready to make complicated plans or charts. All I knew was that I needed to get off the couch because I didn't like how I felt sitting there, day after day, anymore.

One of the best things about my home is the walking path right outside my door. As my feet took steps, some of the cobwebs that had rooted themselves in my brain started clearing out, and I had the first glimmers of creative thoughts I'd had in a long time. In traversing up and down the paths, I came to see how it's possible to recognize where I was out of alignment, look at where I was and where I wanted to go next, and, subsequently, course correct. Getting my nose fixed proved hugely successful: I could breathe! I didn't snore! I could smell! I never realized how poorly my sense of smell worked until I found myself building a scent vocabulary, learning what things smelled like for the first time.

"Oh, that's how lilac smells. How lovely."

Or, "Oh, that's how overcooked fish smells. Why did I do this again?"

It was then that I saw how I could repeat the same process for other parts of life.

When I got home, I felt better than when I left. I was a little more alive, my body tingling and the synapses in my brain firing once again. I was a little sweatier for sure, riding the forgotten endorphin rush that comes from exercise. I felt like I could start my day. It was late afternoon, but better late today than tomorrow or next week.

The next day, sometime in the afternoon, I repeated the process: tying on the running shoes, inserting the earbuds, and hitting the trail. As the days started to pile up, my walks started happening earlier in the day, until it was me and the retired guys on the trail at 6:30 AM, nodding, waving, and smiling at each other every morning. Sure, my pace got faster, the distances grew longer, and the clothes started fitting better. The doctor was happy with the progress I was making and reduced some of the medications I wasn't thrilled to be taking in the first place.

All of that isn't why I tell this story. This essay isn't about what happens when you start your day with a brisk walk. (If you're interested in that topic, may I refer you to the thousands of articles available on Google.) The part that I'd forgotten about was how my creative thoughts never happened in the shower; they popped in my head when I exercised. I amazed myself at the number of ideas I started coming up with on my morning constitutionals. I planned out the early versions of the essay you're reading now on the trail. I'd get the ideas a couple of miles away and hope that I'd hold onto them by the time I got home. Sure, I forgot some, although I remembered and recorded the good ones.

Walking gave me back my creative mojo in ways the simple activity never had before. It's one of the things that helps me keep inertia, anxiety, and depression at bay, leaving me free to tap into my creative juices and share what I can bring to the world.

Now, it's time to look back to the bottom of the grid and see what I want to tackle next. Get back into the dating scene? Maybe. Continue the chase for creative and professional satisfaction? Likely. While I decide, I know I'll have these tools at my disposal and can take the lessons I learned from the trail with me.

Back to the Live Studio Audience:

So, my friend, I told you that story not to brag about having a corner of my life in order, or the fact that I started walking every damn day, or that I'm getting more mileage out of my surgery. All true, except that's not why I told you this story. I told it to illustrate that when I found parts of myself misaligned, it was possible to make a change to grow. The process remains the same:

- Identify the misalignment
- Take stock of your strengths and available resources to address the issues at hand and that are within your agency to address
- Create and implement a plan
- Celebrate the progress and success while getting ready to do it again

My recent examples show that solutions range from things as simple as tying on some shoes and working up a sweat to as complicated as major surgery.

Like life, this hasn't been a perfect or linear process. I'm still prone to anxiety, depression, and panic attacks. I keep up all the other things I do to keep everything in check. It's never one silver bullet; instead, it's a combination of options, tools, and tricks. I wish I could give you the exact mix that will work for you. That's up to you to figure out. Until you figure out what works for you, tying on a pair of trusty sneakers might be a good place to start looking for your lost mojo. I might not suggest major facial surgery for your first conscious foray into this process, but if that's what it takes, who am I to judge?

I leave you with these questions: What's working for you? What needs some improvement? When life gets hard, what's the first step you can take that will get you off your proverbial couch and back to a higher or more creative version of yourself? For me, it's walking and writing with a bottle of water close at hand. What's your starting point? How can you start showing up for yourself so that you cultivate the space to attend to your busy, crazy, artist life?

In the meantime, if you're looking for me early in the morning, you'll most likely find me on the walking trail.

Perpetually curious, **JESSICA H. ROBINSON** is a writer bringing her practical approach, lessons learned, and compassion to help others show up in their personal, professional, and artistic lives more effectively. She currently lives outside Boston, Massachusetts, with her dog Grace, who enjoys taking part in all matters of import.

Betrayal: The Bad Artist's Greatest Act

First Act

There's a story doing the rounds about a male writer who, each day, wandered out of the family home and down the garden path to his writing shed, not to be seen for the rest of the day as he worked diligently away on his book. The family knew not to disturb the man when he was writing. This went on for years. But one day, someone did dare disturb this man, who was also a father and a husband . . . except, when they knocked, no answer came. So, they forced open the door and went inside. What they discovered was this: an empty shed and some loosened boards, torn back just wide enough for a full-grown man to wiggle through. That night, they confronted the man and learned, to their disgust, that he had been sneaking down to the local bar. This was the end of his writing career.

I get how a story like that looks bad—why the family damned him—but I also get why the man lied . . . and how a lie, once told, becomes the whole truth. It takes time to get under the understood. And, as artists, when we cloak ourselves in subterfuge and pretext, the things set up against us from the get-go only harden into misconceptions and gross misunderstanding.

The cover-up wasn't so a man could go to the pub; it was the belief that a creative soul can produce art while sitting eight hours a day in a box, with no human contact, no view, no natural light, just a clock. The cover-up is forever making ourselves out to be fully functioning, paid-up members of society, clocking in and clocking out, when what Art craves is our willingness to loosen the boards and make full-grown space for ourselves. This man's story goes awry not because he was caught out but because, in our culture, compulsiveness, addictiveness, and suffering in pursuit of a product can be tolerated . . . but not time set aside for the unspecified.

When we perpetuate a language of productivity—word counts and hours clocked—to our neighbours, we shrink-wrap our mutual perceptiveness and deny the possibility of transcending the mundane. The real shame is in conceding to our behaviour being "bad," and our "bad behaviour" being tolerated—setting the other up as the good guy (those who tolerate) and ourselves as the bad guys (the tolerated). This makes our lives, and those around us, intolerable, assigning everyone just another role to act out.

Starting out writing fiction, I wrote like a Trojan—like the Greeks were at the gates and could attack any day. I had to get this written, whatever "this" was at the time. There was paid work and there was writing, there were writer groups and there was writing, there was work to pay for writers' retreats where there was writing, and there were relationships that got in the way of writing. Then, one day, I looked up and ten years had passed.

Naturally, that wouldn't do. Time was of the essence, so I quit my job. Maybe then I'd have enough time.

But be prepared! This is no cautionary tale about the woes of not sticking with the day job; no, this next part of the tale is about the hostility your nearest and dearest will exhibit in the face of your newfound aimlessness. It turns out time is never the obstacle; attitudes are.

Valiantly (so it must have seemed to them), people attempted to correct my behaviour, get me back on track, deeming that "society knows best for me." When I questioned the merits of their prescription, they threw their hands up in despair. They thought what they were doing was kind—there was a me, and then there was a behaviour. The fact that I couldn't respect how they were targeting the behaviour, and not me, was part of my problem.

What they never allowed was how their interventions didn't arrive in isolation—no, there was nowhere I could go for respite; they became the wall insisting there was no place else to go.

But they were wrong. There was another place I could go: down.

To the outside world, depression may seem the ultimate act of self-pity. What those around us cannot fathom is that this disturbance is no act, but the baseline of defeat. When you have no reserves left, the reproaches your nearest and dearest can and will aim at you are formidable . . . and when you have strangely lost all feeling for life, your feelings for them do not go away. With enough application, they finally get you to stop making this about you; instead, it gets to be how bad you're making them feel, and when you're going to stop. And the walled circle is complete.

In that moment, when you realize you're closed in on all sides, you begin the slow crawl back to going along to get along. You take the antidepressants, apply for a job, get a place to live, pay your taxes. Only now you know what you're doing is not to be a burden, and whatever was left of your fine spirit trails elsewhere.

But before that happened, there was a moment between giving up and returning to a faded version of a life. That was when I entertained a flurry of writing, a last burst of creativity before shutting up shop for years as a writer. It was the closest I came to the vicinity of myself in over a year. But feeling good, exultant even, felt dangerous—for no one, least of all me, gets to override the simple math: contribution is monetary. I couldn't do this fast enough, and so it couldn't be.

Soon I was back on the societal track: working in a lowly position in public relations at a publishing company in the rural back of beyond, a few warehouses down from the local sewage plant. Lunchtimes, I sat with my colleagues around a bench in a dog park, listening to a twentysomething woman speak about baby showers and motherhood being the sole defining reason for any woman's existence, and feeling so very far away, so very small, so very quiet.

It took five more years, the death of my mother, and recognizing how the harm done to me was not isolated, to finally reach a place where I could hear the muse's valiant calls to return, stronger and truer than all the voices that told me what they thought was best. There was power in discerning that my feelings existed for good reason—pushing me, pulling me, to get to the other side of that wall. For, incredibly, what if a projection is not ours alone—but belongs to others also—that others are trying to meet us in a place beyond the walls the rational will build?

What I do next is not rational: I make a second major hole in my life and wiggle through it. This time, I do not set out to be tolerated; I set out to be the most trustworthy person in my life, the one I find tolerable. Surface level, I understood I was trying to escape the burden of the marketplace—that of only being a worker, a consumer, a tax-paying citizen. Ironically, the arrival of a coveted publishing deal would only have locked me further into this abysmal state. I would forever have remained in a state of anxiety and fear. Because, before I could fulfill my roles as a consumer, citizen, or artist, I first needed to feel like a human being. A realization like that takes time and awareness and, yes, distance—not to be cruel, but somehow more merciful.

It took years to call myself a writer. It took years more to recognize that my writing best rose to meet me, and me the writing, when I was guided by a desire to create Art. When you're creating Art, you cannot bypass certain cornerstones:

The bad artist is non-transactional.

The bad artist doesn't deal in immediate returns.

The bad artist dares to go slow.

The bad artist doesn't collaborate; they consult with.

The bad artist will not be tolerated.

A Second Act

The second time around I practise "care" for myself. Now I am prepared for the backlash. The more I show myself care, respect, trust, patience, loyalty, love, honesty, empathy, and mercy, the more others act out around me. It becomes a battlefield on the home front and away. But I am too far gone to back down. I warn my nearest and dearest that unless I can swivel some of my gentler qualities toward myself, all they will ever know again is backlash.

Some heed my call. Others don't. So be it.

In a place of aggression, gentleness is an act of betrayal.
—"The Fifth Direction" by Tamie Parker Song

I tune into my intuition, and that is the greatest creative breakthrough of all. Suddenly, what once felt like interference becomes a field for creative insights. What is the surrounding situation showing me? How is it playing into the question of what Art is asking of me and what I'm asking of Her? How can this bear fruit?

The root of *interference*: *inter* (among together; involving two or more) and *inference* (bringing in).

Whatever is going on around me isn't getting in the way; it *is* the Way.

I practise foresight, insight, and hindsight. This is not accounting "for" myself, or even "to" myself, but attending to the self and what she needs to do next. I go for long walks. I read, I journal, I observe my daily routine, discover my process, how I dip in and out. I learn not to give myself a hard time, recognizing that I am tending the seed when I am not interfering with the soil.

Reason tells me that when I begin to cultivate and nurture any of these values, my own insecurities, fears, and doubts will arise to test the strength of my commitment and to stretch my capacity. Every test has a benefit merged in with it. What needs to be understood during these battles is that I must not shrink my capacity to trust.

Fourth, I restore balance by honouring and asserting my inner qualities (intuition, feelings, and perception) while not sacrificing reason (my intellect and the facts). I still do the accounts and the housework, keep informed about the news, but externals are no longer internalized. I am no longer spun out by the ways of the world. I acclimate to what I can do in the moment, according to my strength and abilities.

In order not to betray myself again, I must prize integrity higher than others prize loyalty. That becomes the root. I exercise no iron-fisted control over others. I simply will not deny myself the source of my own strength.

Revelation

I discover that what I have tapped into is not in isolation. Gayatri Naraine, a representative at the UN, defines such an approach under the banner of "The Feminine Principle."

> Looking outside myself is the way to let loose waves of victimization, uncertainty, and insecurity and so feelings are often suppressed and never dealt with. This suppression of feelings leads to depression as I am unable to trust my own feelings and I am reluctant to talk about them, fearing being misunderstood, criticized, or rejected. Staying close to my own truth, innate values, and inner strength enables me to trust my feelings, keep an "eye" on "I."[1]

Confirmation

Aldous Huxley spoke of a Law of Reversed Effort:

> The harder we try with conscious will to do something,
> the less we shall succeed. Proficiency, and the results
> of proficiency, come only to those who have learned
> the paradoxical art of doing and not doing, or com-
> bining relaxation with activity, of letting go so that the
> immanent and transcendent Unknown Quantity may
> take hold.[2]

We cannot make ourselves understand. The most we can do is to foster a state of mind in which understanding may come to us.

Resist All Calls to Hastiness

I'm back here, in this space before writing, trying to resist all calls to hastiness, which some days feels more counterintuitive than others. But here I am, holding space, trying not to amplify and magnify multiple renditions of "hurry up." I wait to know my next move. While I'm waiting, I come across a passage from a random early fiction draft. There, buried inside, is a guiding note in enlarged caps and deep red font: INTENTION. ONE FLOOR AT A TIME. BUT REMEMBER PEOPLE ARE DROWNING AND THERE'S A FIRE. TIME IS OF THE ESSENCE. COMPLETE THE DISCOVERIES TO UNDERSTAND THE TRICKS. FOR ONLY ONCE THE TRICKS ARE UNDERSTOOD WILL THE WAY BE CLEARED FOR THE TRAILS.

What leaps out at me: "people are drowning," "there's a fire," and "time is of the essence," confirming my worst nightmare: I didn't make it in time to help anyone. If only I could have written this sooner, got this out sooner.

All of a sudden, it dawns on me: What conceit! My rushing is predicated on the belief that I get to play hero. Where does this come from? Look what harm it does, is doing. I read those capped letters again, and this time what stands out is "intention," "one floor at a time," and "of the essence." I remind myself that I am not writing this in the public domain. I am writing within these four walls, and with a duty of care to these characters.

If I panic now, how is that of help to anyone, least of all me?

Conclusion

Over time, I have learned to trust the creative act itself. That faith has been met in real terms. Doubt happens: we forget our own advice, we grow hasty. But much like the layering of acetates, the work calls for this extra layering of care to what life is gesturing, signalling.

I can't stop now. I will go all the way. And it will take as long as it takes.

Author of *33 Walks in London*, NICOLA PERRY began her publishing career as a fiction editor with Amazon and head of editorial services for Bloomsbury's Writers & Artists. With a Master's (with distinction) in Poetics of Imagination from Dartington College, England, Nicola is well-versed in herstory and mythology, poetic thinking and the creative process. Her passion, though, is cultural witnessing of the Female Gaze; not in film studies terms but with a nod to Consciousness and cognitive studies.

LINDA BROWNE

The Murakami Method: Rewriting Long Covid

Prologue

On March 24, 2020, I contract Covid-19.

It's a date that's been burned into my mind and body in ways science hasn't totally figured out. At the time, I only know that I'm sick. A bewildering array of symptoms courses through my body for weeks. What I remember most from that time is an overwhelming feeling of erasure—as if Covid-19 had rubbed out the person I had been and left in its place a smudged and blurred stranger. Still, I feel lucky to be alive.

As a writer, I'm desperate to get back to work, but a curious numbness descends, as if the writing part of me has gone dormant or perhaps been put to sleep. After spending nearly three weeks in bed, unable to write, I am clearly out of practice. I'm certain that I can rebuild my writing routine in the same way that I'm rebuilding my strength. Like my body, my writing self will soon recover. I'm still a writer, after all. It's the one thing I'm sure of.

First Draft

In late April, I pick up a manuscript I'd been working on before I got sick. Months before the pandemic, one of my clients had introduced me to a literary agent. I didn't have a finished manuscript at the time, but the introduction was an incredible opportunity, too good to pass up. So I sent a query letter and writing sample. I made it clear that I was still working on a first draft. To my surprise, the agent told me to send her the manuscript when it was "as good as I could make it."

What did that mean? I was painfully green at the publishing game and hadn't always been able to read between the lines of the professional comments I was starting to receive. Was "take your time" some kind of industry code for "get it to me as soon as possible?" Surely, a year wasn't an acceptable timeline (although secretly, I thought it was what my book needed). In a year, the agent would have forgotten all about me. Better try for six months. That would show the agent I was a Serious Writer who could get work done.

Instead of sending the agent a note to say that I was recovering from Covid-19 and needed more time with the manuscript, I decide to keep to my original schedule. That I'd decided to ignore my own internal sense of what the manuscript needed should have sent up a huge red flag. It didn't.

The first anomaly shows up early. During my first post-Covid writing session, I can only write for two hours—less than my usual three or four. Over the next few days, the pattern of writing becomes more erratic: one day, I write for one hour, the next day three hours, followed by two, two-hour days, then a day of nothing. On Nothing Day, I completely lose track of time. I can't even say where the day has gone. I put it all down to warming up after a lengthy break, but the pattern persists. I block out time, I go to my writing room but can't focus on anything. I haven't varied my routine: I still set the same timers, I take the same breaks, but a dull, grey fog infiltrates my mind and steals away the immersive concentration I need to enter my characters' worlds and tell their stories. At the end of each day, I rise from my chair, coated with the dust of disappointment and struggle:

I'm ashamed of how little I wrote today. I feel like every-
thing I'm writing is CRAP. Am I working this book to
death? Can I write it at all?
YES. I CAN.
It's really, really hard to focus if I'm at all interrupted.
Or maybe my focus is just shot anyway.

At night, I can't sleep for more than two or three hours at a time. I awake abruptly, with a pounding heart and a brain full of snow. Worries and questions swarm around me, spiralling into full-blown anxiety. Like many writers, I'm used to viewing the world through a lens of cautious introversion, but this is full-on panic—not only about writing but everything else that pops into my mind. Worse, I can't even read a book to put myself back to sleep. Whenever I try to read, the words on the page slip sideways. I can't hold onto their meaning. This cycle lasts for two or three hours every night. My brain is on fire, and there is nothing I can do to put it out.

I write in shorter and shorter blocks. Revisions are usually my favourite part of writing, but there is nothing joyful about the work I bang out in those fifteen- or twenty-minute blocks when I can claw my mind free of the fog. On Saturday, May 9, 2020, I finally complete my manuscript with a niggling sense of unease: I don't have any feeling for the story. I usually know when a story is "finished," but this time, nothing.

Friends tell me not to worry. A pandemic malaise had taken hold of them as well. Everybody is anxious and depressed and un-productive. Other writers are finding it difficult to read and write, too. I tell myself that all will come back to me once I finally clear this clotted web of unfocused distraction. As more time passes, I find this harder and harder to believe.

In late May 2020, I finally bundle my submission off to the agent and three writing contests. The agent says she's busy and plans to get to my manuscript soon. One of the writing contests asks for my full manuscript. At least I can still write a pitch. More time passes with a no from the writing contests and radio silence from the agent. Either I can't write or there's a major problem with the manuscript. Chastened and ashamed, I reach out to a former writing mentor for help.

During a Zoom meeting, my mentor's kind enough to walk me through multiple scenes before revealing, as gently as possible, that I've got no story—just a series of scenes that don't make any narrative sense. The fact that I failed to complete a well-structured story and sent out a series of unordered scenes—not once but four times—without being able to tell the difference fills me with dread. How could I have done such a thing?

A horrible suspicion enters my mind. What if Covid-19 somehow evolved into a whole new set of symptoms? The disease has already racked my body with pain and fatigue, squeezed the air out of my lungs, and made my heart race for no reason. It's robbed me of sleep with nightly panic attacks. What if Covid's invaded my brain?

Revise

For me, neurological symptoms and swiftly deteriorating cognitive ability in the space of a few weeks come as a huge shock. I have no way to frame this experience. The official discovery of long Covid is still in the future. As a first wave survivor, I'm ahead of the science. One of my favourite writers, Audre Lorde, speaks of the body as both a guide and a tool. In my case, the tool is broken and my inner guide has vanished into the fog. I thought I was healing, but I'd drawn a wild card and a joker was floating around in my mind. Unlike most essential workers, I'm fortunate enough to have savings and recovery benefits that allow me to stay at home. I'm also a writer who's lost the ability to write. Who knows when I'll get it back? Or if I will at all?

To Audre Lorde, the answer to this question is found in the

body itself, in felt experience rooted in daily living. As it turns out, Covid agrees with her.[1] Compared to my brain, my body is starting to recover, though my energy levels fluctuate wildly. Each day has to be mapped out according to new criteria: how much energy do I have, and where do I most need to spend it? This is a question I ask myself at the start of each day over the next year. It turns out the answer has nothing to do with writing.

Political scientist and war zone survivor, Dr. Aisha Ahmad, draws some important parallels between surviving a pandemic and a war. To Ahmad, it's vital that people recognize they're not the same person they were in the Before Times, and that productivity is a "hyper-reaction" to losing all control over your own life. Far from being a writer's retreat, a deadly pandemic is a time to take control of our individual critical infrastructure. For those of us who are either sick or recovering from the virus, it's a time to heal.[2]

And go for a walk, preferably in a park.

According to Ahmad, going for a walk not only provides essential exercise but a daily opportunity to shift our thinking as we learn to accept what a changed world offers us. Walking helps us not to focus on the new restrictions, the things we can no longer do or the loss of what we once had. Rather, it allows us to navigate our way through the crisis and set ourselves up to transition into what comes next.

Take your cues from daily lived experience, no matter how new and how fraught it is, learn how to shift your perceptions to accept a changed world on its own terms. It's like Aisha Ahmad sat down with Audre Lorde at a safe physical distance, maybe on a park bench, to share fundamental survival tactics. I won't come across Ahmad's work for another eight months, but like many first wave Covid survivors, my reality has already shifted.

In July 2020, I feel well enough to take on a temporary job and suffer a major relapse. I respond by scaling back. Each day, I wake up at the same time, shower, get dressed, make some good, nutritious food to eat, spend time with my partner, and go to bed early. However much I try to reign myself in, my new "don't push" mantra doesn't entirely work. My body is recovering faster than my brain. I'm in that weird healing period where I need to increase my daily activity in order to tire myself out enough so I can dodge my anxious brain and get some sleep. It's a delicate balancing act. I take it slow, feeling my way:

> *I think one thing to watch carefully is pacing. When I feel good, I tend to default back to doing too much. Then I get tired, and it's hard to dig out of that. I need to leave something in the tank, build up reserves. And I need to keep going. I'm driven to excel but maybe that drive can be harnessed in a different direction.*

On days when I'm fatigued, I rest. If my energy is good, I gently test out the limits of what I can do. By August, I'm able to set up a garden at my best friend's house.

My writing is slower to recover. The anxious voices at night still prod me into wakefulness. Peace and equilibrium continue to elude me. As a writer living with cognitive impairment, I wonder what this radically altered reality means. The standard writing advice is to write every day, no matter what. Whoever invented that rule obviously never had to deal with Covid-induced brain fog. The reality is that my mind wanders off in a thousand different directions so that it's almost impossible to focus and concentrate. For the first time, it occurs to me that I might have to completely stop writing in order to be able to continue at all.

For the next three weeks, I stop trying to force myself to do something I can't. The relief is intense and palpable. I feel like I can psychically breathe again. After a week of this routine, I can tolerate reading short articles but not books. I toss out my three to four books per month habit. Yet, I'm still hungry for stories. What

I need is a new way of thinking about storytelling. I haven't lost my ability to listen so I decide to switch from books to audiobooks and podcasts. I seize on anything and everything that piques my interest. I listen to a lot of nonfiction. Listening in my own genre is too painful, a reminder of everything I've lost. I temporarily turn my back on middle grade and young adult fiction.

On week four, I sit down again in my writing chair. My Type-A self is eager to race ahead, but by this time, I know what surrendering to that impulse will cost me. Instead, I lower the bar on my expectations. Instead of pushing myself to write for three or four hours at a time, I set a half-hour timer. I manage fifteen minutes before my concentration breaks and my mind floats away. I take a ten-minute break, then come back to my chair. Another fifteen minutes, and I'm done for the day. I try not to cry as I shut down the computer. It feels like I've given up on writing and that writing has given up on me. I tell myself I'm trying to rebuild my brain, not finish a manuscript.

The next day, I try again for another half-hour. The same thing happens. Next day, I try again. Same result. Every day, I show up and set that half-hour timer. I don't force myself to work on the book at all. Right now, I have no ambitions. I'm just trying to write. Some days, I can manage some words. On other days, the fatigue and fog roll in, zapping my strength and filling my mind with dragonfly thoughts. Concentration flits away. On those days, I direct all available resources to self-care—including walks.

What is emerging, slowly, is a new way of seeing the world and my place in it. The first jolt of dissonance between the person I was in the Before Times and a still-emergent self slams into me during an acceptance speech given by *The Great British Baking Show*'s 2015 winner, Nadiya Hussain. On camera, Nadiya fiercely dismantles the internal barriers that have held her back, promising never to put boundaries around herself that limit what she thinks she can do. She'll never try to talk herself out of something ahead of time by either not committing to it, or by saying she can't do it. She can do it, and she will.[3]

Nadiya's speech resonates powerfully with a lot of people. For me, her words—and her determination—open an emotional floodgate. I cry for my mangled mind, the person and writer I once was. Aisha Ahmad describes the loss that occurs before growth, the dry time before a new creative period begins. I'm terrified as I look across a life devoid of the things that once defined me, especially writing, which has dried to a trickle. All around me is shifting sand, with no solid ground. And yet, Nadiya's conviction resonates like a small, unexpected flower.

Toronto, Huron Street Public School, 1970s

I arrive in my Grade 5 classroom one morning to find that our teacher, Mrs. Murakami, has made a wall planner for each of us. Every morning after hanging up our coats and depositing our lunch boxes in the cloak room, Mrs. Murakami tells us, we will use these planners to map out our individual work for the day.

For me, the wall planner becomes a place of revelation and experimentation where I can figure out the "hows" of working for myself. Mrs. Murakami must have guided us, helped us, and held us accountable for completing our tasks. All I remember is how I raced to that planner every morning, eager to arrange my cards in just the right order for that day. If I changed my mind as I went along, I could easily rearrange the cards. I remember the way working like this made me feel: powerful, in charge of my own life. Transformed.

Rewrite

As December 31, 2020, merges with the bruised dawn of a new year, it is Mrs. Murakami's organizing method I turn to for help. I've carried it with me for years, and it's a big reason why I use bullet journals today. The Murakami Method is like a bullet journal but looser. It's a map for how the day might unfold with plenty of room for changes. I list all the activities that now count as writing practice, including listening to audiobooks. I also list the other tasks I'm able to complete each day. I'm struck by their sheer number. They add up to so much more than I could even imagine doing nine months ago.

Still, recovery from Covid-induced brain fog is cyclical, not linear. I'm immersed inside a changing, unfamiliar body. I never really know where I stand on any given day. The Murakami Method creates a framework of basic expectations around each day, but the cards are mine to shuffle and deal. On some days, I can actually write for one, two, or even three hours. Other days completely slip away from me. On those days, when I find myself standing in my pyjamas with no idea of where the time has gone, I start with self-care: shower, dress, prepare something simple and healthy to eat. Instead of writing, I might listen to a podcast or audiobook, go for a walk, put on a load of laundry, do the dishes, anything to get me moving and break the inertia. Later, I will find out that Dr. Aisha Ahmad uses this exact same technique to rescue a train-wrecked day. She recommends keeping the to-do list basic on these days, and to ease back into a modest amount of more complex tasks on the following day. Audre Lorde, sitting on the park bench in my mind, nods her head. In her essay, "The Uses of the Erotic: The Erotic as Power," she warns against conflating the internal demands for excellence with demanding the impossible, as such a requirement incapacitates everyone in the process.[4]

We're often told as writers that we must push through resistance and blocks at all costs, but trying to push an injured brain or punishing myself for non-performance seems counterproductive and damaging. So I don't push. I pace. I don't focus on what my hyped-up writing self thinks I should do. Instead, I reshuffle the cards to find some movement—any movement—forward. I stand at ground zero of a long-haul recovery with eyes that see myself and the world very differently from the way I did in the Before Times. The Murakami Method shines like a beacon through the persistent fog. It doesn't show me the way back to myself; that self is gone, swept away by a disease we're only just starting to understand. Yet, I find the key to rebuilding my present lies in the past: in a Grade 5 classroom where Mrs. Murakami taught me a way of seeing, a flexibility that allows me to creatively adapt to changing circumstances and dodge self-judgment when my expectations fall short.

On difficult days, on good days, I keep on shuffling the cards, creating forward momentum, bit by bit. The scary truth is, I don't know if I'll ever be able to write in the ways that I used to. I haven't arrived at this place empty-handed, though. I've got skills that let me salvage my power and agency from the ruin of fog-bound days. On those days when my mind is clear (and there are increasingly more of them), I've got the tools to recreate what writing can look like inside this changed self. I'm in the transition, walking with shaky legs on unfamiliar ground. Inside this ending is a solid beginning. That's more than enough for me.

Then, one morning in June 2021, I look up from my writing and realize that an hour and a half has flown by. I'd forgotten to set my timer. I was too immersed in the story to notice.

LINDA BROWNE is an author of (mostly) middle grade and young adult Science Fiction Fantasy. Her work has been longlisted in The Times/Chicken House Children's Fiction Competition and she's also been a finalist in CANSCAIP's Writing for Children Competition. Her debut middle grade steampunk novel, *Shadow Apprentice*, was published in spring 2024. Linda lives in Toronto with her partner, and far too many books and plants.

II

We're All Mad Here

Can you picture her?

I try to imagine my grandmother as I never knew her: a young woman with bright red hair and a familiar upper lip, walking into the Academy of Fine Arts in Warsaw after the end of the world.

Until recently, it never occurred to me that I might be chronically unwell. In fact, I actively rejected the idea, particularly after I was first diagnosed with a clinical anxiety disorder when I was fourteen. It was 2004 and, in some significant ways, our collective attitudes around mental health had more in common with the last century than this one.

In 2004, my immediate family members were the only people I knew who went to therapy, but my parents resisted the idea of psychiatric medications—especially for children. The shame I felt after being diagnosed with generalized anxiety disorder was so deeply internalized that my illness also became my biggest secret. When I had to miss school regularly for treatment, I panicked about how to explain my many absences to friends and teachers. I hated the ways my brain and body responded to the world, and I soon started to hate myself.

"Would you hate yourself if you had cancer?" my mother asked rhetorically. "Of course not. It's an illness. It isn't you. Hate the cancer. Hate the anxiety, not yourself."

I started to think of anxiety and panic attacks like tumours, something I could irradiate or cut out. If the treatment was successful, they might never come back again. I focused everything I could on overcoming my "disease."

At the end of my treatment at the Hospital for Sick Children, my psychologist said I was the "poster child" for the program.

At sixteen, I decided I was in remission, and I was determined to stay there for the rest of my life.

In my family, two truths were never explained because they were always taken for granted.

The First Truth: Our family makes art and tells stories. We don't talk about why, or whether it is a good use of time, or if creating has value of any kind. If you're alive, you make things.

The Second Truth: Anxiety disorders, mood disorders, and intergenerational trauma are woven tightly into our little family. We don't need to ask where our mental illness came from, it came from the end of the world.

My grandmother, a professional graphic designer and visual artist, continued to make art into her nineties. Only when confined to a hospital bed in the last three weeks of her life, did she stop painting.

My mental images of my grandmother's life are like her paintings: loose brushstrokes evoke a subject that is both easily recognizable and impressionistic. The eras that defined and divided her life each become a canvas in my mind. Only recently have I started to look more closely at the gaps between them: there is blank space between 1945 and 1950, when my grandmother began to study at the Academy of Fine Arts.

After she passed away, I became haunted by the question I had never thought to ask her: *Nana, why did you decide to be an artist?*

"Make art, then die," my first art teacher told our Grade 9 class.

A few years later, at least three of my classmates had the phrase tattooed on their bodies.

Creativity demands space. Space of every kind. A room, a studio, a landscape. A space of time otherwise unclaimed. Financial space.

I have never been very good at claiming space for myself, which I think is partly why I decided to do my undergraduate degree in theatre instead of creative writing. Theatre is about taking up space. You are allowed—expected—to follow your impulses, to express yourself fully, to dance and sing and grasp and leap when words aren't enough. You excel only when you embody what's inside you, step even more fully into yourself, stand tall and say, "Here I am." I learned so much of what I needed to know about art and life in theatre school. It gave me an empty space and invited me to fill it with anything true and nothing but myself.

My undergraduate years were also some of my best mental health years. I wasn't in therapy or on medication. I believed in myself and the work I was doing. I barely thought about anxiety or panic attacks except as something I had dealt with in the past.

I graduated, moved to downtown Toronto, and spent most of that summer crying in Kensington Market.

I went back to therapy, I started taking an ssri, and I tried not to think about it. Throughout my twenties, no matter what happened in my life or my health, my family's first universal truth remained constant: if you're alive, you make things.

So, I did.

If nature abhors a vacuum, then the empty space required to create is particularly vulnerable. There is always something more important to do, something more worthwhile, more practical, more lucrative. Something less selfish. Anyone who has ever tried to make anything has likely experienced the roar of life rushing in to fill the empty space with any one of its other responsibilities. As a writer with mood and anxiety disorders, the space I need to create is also a place where mental illness can flood in.

But here's the thing: When you create, you make something that did not exist before. Something that takes up space.

This is what I did for most of my life, without even realizing it. I wrote and sang and drew in part to keep the disorders away.

A fridge magnet in my father's kitchen:

Alice laughed. "There's no use trying," she said; "one can't believe impossible things."

"I daresay you haven't had much practice," said the Queen. "When I was younger, I always did it for half an hour a day. Why sometimes I've believed as many as six impossible things before breakfast."

I experienced my first major depressive episode in early 2020. It was a few months after the publication of my first book, and a few months before my thirtieth birthday. The depression began before the first lockdown, but it was exacerbated and deepened by the fear, uncertainty, and social isolation that followed. I was living alone for the first time and had fallen out of love with Toronto. I believed I had nothing meaningful left to contribute to the world.

The first thing I lost was my ability to read. My eyes would go over and over the same phrase, understanding the words but unable to hold their collective meaning together in my mind long enough to move on to the next sentence.

Then I dropped my journaling routine. There was nothing to do, nothing to remember, nothing to write about or scrapbook or draw.

I stopped crocheting, stopped learning to sew. Buying yarn and fabric off the internet seemed irresponsible and wasteful when the planet was dying, and I had a closet full of clothes I couldn't wear anyway.

I am still struggling to understand depression, let alone write about it. I want to write that being depressed was like sleeping for three years, but that's not right. My experience was not of disengaging with the world, but of being wide awake and severed from myself. My family's first universal truth seemed like nothing more than a fantasy, and I felt like a fool for having built so much of my life upon it. I wondered if any of my former classmates regretted their tattoos.

If writing about depression is difficult, writing about emerging from it is only slightly easier. I got a kitten. I reread my favourite novels, the ones I nearly have memorized, until I could grasp prose properly again. I admitted that I was not, and never had been, "cured." I started to process the realization that I had never been fully diagnosed or sufficiently treated. I found an excellent psychiatrist to stick with me for the long haul, and I started the slow climb back to myself.

The simple truth is that I got better with treatment. It is also true that the process is opaque, disheartening, and ambiguous. I had to start thinking differently about the nature of treatment itself. The fact that I was able to access the proper treatment at all was mostly a combination of privilege and luck.

I have become afraid of my quiet mind. Afraid of the empty space I used to create in so easily. Anxiety and depression are now too eager to fill that vacuum. I have found most of myself again, but writing is still not nearly as easy as it used to be.

Mental illness is its own kind of apocalypse. Depression. Trauma. Mania. Nothing makes sense when reality as you know it ceases to exist. Sometimes it seems like madness is the only possible response to the insanity of the world.

Describing myself as a writer whose ability to create has been compromised by illness is very difficult for me. It feels like some kind of medical appropriation, disrespectful to everyone living with an incurable medical diagnosis to count myself among them. Then I remember I have several incurable diagnoses.

Nevertheless, I am well. I am lucky and grateful. As I go about my days, I don't think of myself as anything other than healthy, but I am still learning to accept my weird and wonderful brain.

And I'm learning to believe in art again.

Nana, how did you believe, after 1939, that art matters at all?

An old art history textbook catches my eye every so often when I walk into the living room or pick a cat up off the bookshelf. The title is boring and the print is small, but it is one of the few textbooks I have chosen to keep. It is an accessible introduction to thirteen avant-garde art movements from the early twentieth century. Taken together, these overviews of Surrealism, Dada, and Absurdism—to name a few—tell me a powerful story:

The world has ended countless times before. When nothing matters and reality no longer exists, we create something new.

I think about getting a tattoo.

It may look like madness from the outside, but if we're still alive, we make things.

NELLWYN LAMPERT is a writer, editor, bookseller, and teacher. She is the author of *Every Boy I Ever Kissed* (Dundurn Press, 2019) and holds an MFA in Creative Nonfiction. Nellwyn has written or edited for CBC *First Person, She Does the City, The Huffington Post,* and *The Ex-Puritan Literary Magazine,* among others. She has taught creative writing and communications, having served as an instructor at Seneca Polytechnic and King's Writing Workshops. As a bookseller, she is dedicated to helping children develop a love of reading and finding the perfect book for every reader.

Just to Be

The door swung open as my fist still hung in the air, poised to knock. The tall, thin woman in front of me smiled beneath her face mask. She sported shoulder-cropped blond hair, mascara-lined caramel eyes, and thin-rimmed oval glasses. She wore long, flowy pants and a billowing linen top. She could've been an artist, perhaps a painter; watercolour.

She was my therapist.

"Would you like a glass of water?" she asked, inviting me into her warmly lit living room. The evening sun spilled in through a dining room window. A glass coffee table holding a box of tissues was thoughtfully placed next to a beige couch loaded with rotund pillows. "No, but can I use your washroom?" I asked, my stomach tightening. I didn't want to have to pee in the middle of my first counselling session.

It took me eight years to start therapy. You'd think, being the proactive planner that I am, I would've jumped in sooner to just get it over with, outlining a time-bound checklist for healing from grief: a progression through the stages of denial, guilt, bargaining, depression.

But I was only twenty years old when I suffered a life-changing injury and an irrevocable loss, and I wasn't ready to talk to a stranger about my problems. Those days were filled with doctor's appointments, relearning how to walk in physiotherapy, and re-reading the last messages I would ever receive from my dad.

Most mornings, I'd push myself out of bed and struggle into the shower, the hot water a respite on my hypersensitive scars. My mom would come in when I called her, razor in hand, to shave my legs since I couldn't bend down to reach. I'd cower behind the plastic curtain, not wanting her to see my naked body or my stitched-up back. "Can you hurry up?" I'd ask, biting back tears of embarrassment.

After fracturing my spine while travelling through Europe, I'd returned home to Canada on a stretcher. Almost immediately afterwards, my father was killed in a workplace accident. My spontaneous, carefree youth fractured into "before" and "after."

Knowing the deep emotional pain that I was engulfed in, my mom booked me an appointment with a well-respected grief counsellor a few weeks later, but on the arranged date, I refused to go. I didn't want to talk about my dad's sudden death or my broken back. It was too fresh; it wasn't real to me yet. Talking about it might make it real.

Eight years after my accident, I could hike, dance, and travel, although without the massive 50-litre backpack I used to lug around. My back would often ache, forcing me to lie down and rest, but I was grateful to be able to move, exercise, and even snowboard again.

One beautiful February day, I was cautiously hiking along a trail that was covered in slippery mounds of ice, bubbling up like uneven scoops of ice cream. My boyfriend, Tavis, paused while I caught up to him. Our hiking partners were almost out of sight behind the evergreens.

We were hiking back from Norvan Falls near Vancouver, British Columbia. As usual, my partner was carrying the backpack, our shared water and snacks resting upon his shoulders rather than weighing down my weak spine.

After two invasive spinal surgeries, I'd learned to listen to my body. I slowed down, took pictures of the scenery, and rested beside turquoise lakes while others climbed cliffs and jumped in. I knew I was lucky to be walking at all. But sometimes, I wanted to be able to keep up. I wanted to feel normal, not one step away from hurting myself again.

Slipping off an icy boardwalk, I felt my ankle twist in. My knee buckled. "Ouch!" I cried. I leaned my weight on Tavis's shoulder, rubbing my knee and fighting tears. We still had at least five kilometres to go.

"Take your time," Tavis said. I looked up; our adventure buddies were long gone.

Wincing in pain, I limped back to the trailhead. At home, I placed a bag of frozen peas on my knee and elevated it to decrease the swelling.

Then Covid hit.

My weekend adventures came to a screeching halt, and my knee pain receded. I figured I'd healed. The last thing I needed was another long-term injury. I already knew what it was to be broken.

When I finally booked my first therapy appointment, my dad's death and my own back injury still felt fresh. Eight years hadn't dulled the scars and loss; the heartache and regret. Despite my past, I lived a happy life as a journalist and editor for an outdoor adventure magazine. I wrote travel stories and freelance articles. During my Master of Fine Arts program, I wrote a manuscript for a book about losing my dad, breaking my back, and travelling the world.

As I wrote, tears poured out of my eyes like the West Coast rain. I descended into fits of hiccups and suffered panic attacks; I took breaks to watch silly cat videos and stretch my back in yoga classes. As anxiety-inducing as it was, something inside me broke with relief. Telling my story was therapeutic. Writing out the pain was like gulping down a deep breath of fresh air after surviving on low oxygen.

There wasn't a grand sign in the sky that convinced me to start therapy, just a lingering curiosity somewhere below the painful memories. Hearing my friends talk about their dads. Stumbling on old pictures of my family, arms wrapped around each other on sepia-tinted vacations. I found a counsellor who had a soothing voice and offered hope of moving on. A few sessions should heal my heart, I thought. No more than five. Maybe six.

That summer, Tavis and I were hiking down from the Stawamus Chief, an epic mountain just outside of Squamish, when my knee crumpled again.

It started as a prickling sensation, grew to an uncomfortable ache, then howled with gnawing pain. I hobbled down the final steps of a wooden staircase, trying to place most of my weight on my other leg. With a sense of deja vu, I iced my knee and made an appointment with a physiotherapist. Already, in my mind, I was planning: see the physiotherapist, fix my knee, get back to hiking. I was going to be okay. I had to be.

At my first counselling session, I perched on the edge of the sand-coloured couch and spoke about my past, trying not to feel like a mental patient up for evaluation.

My therapist responded by offering reassurances—"You've been through a lot"—and asking questions: "What emotions are you most comfortable with?" I talked about my pain, fear, sadness, confusion, loss of innocence and identity. "The only emotion you haven't mentioned is anger," she noted.

I thought about it before responding, "Women aren't supposed to be angry," and realizing just how damn infuriated I was.

I squeezed my hands into fists as my left knee twinged while I reclined on the bed at my physiotherapist's office days later. She leaned over my body, forcing needles into muscles that caused little spasms. Her silky black hair was pulled back into a low ponytail. She reminded me to breathe; I forced my palms together and felt cold, clammy sweat.

After every appointment, she emailed me long lists of exercises I rarely executed perfectly. Boredom and discomfort crept in quickly, stopping me from sticking to a schedule. "You should have time to do these," she said, hands on her hips. I nodded, silently reprimanding myself for watching Netflix and doomscrolling when I should've been doing my physio exercises. Time ticked by, and I didn't see any improvement.

I hated my knee. My physiotherapist corrected me when I called it my "bad" knee. "It's your rehabbing knee," she said. "Let's call it that instead."

It sounded nice, but it didn't make it hurt any less. Even when I sat at my desk and wrote, even when I relaxed in bed and read, I could feel my kneecap pulsing. "Getting older sucks," I would say to my friends, laughing when I needed to excuse my body's limitations, but it wasn't really a joke.

Before fracturing my spine, I was a risk-taker: I went bungee jumping in New Zealand, paragliding in Austria, and scuba diving in Bali. I was backpacking solo when I broke my back. I changed from an independent world traveller to a vigilant young adult, desperate to take charge of my future and create the life I'd always dreamed of, yet afraid my plans were already unachievable.

"You desire control, because you had none," my therapist told me. "With your back injury. With your dad's death."

"Can I get to a place where I feel comfortable being out of control?" I asked, trying to picture how it would look: relinquishing the need to be the one to make every dinner reservation; to write down my daily schedule hour by hour; to send detailed grocery shopping lists to Tavis. How can I be sure I won't forget? How can I trust someone else will do it right?

She assured me change is possible, that it starts in the mind, and trickles out to behaviour. She spoke patiently, listening to my excuses.

Finally, she proposed somatic work to release my anger. We stood across the living room from one another. She lifted the glass coffee table out of the way, and I avoided her gaze as my back ached.

In her loose pants and signature linen top, she mirrored my stance: arms dangling, legs spread hip distance apart, feet firmly grounded. "Close your eyes, and try to feel within your body," she said. She began breathing, inhaling like the sound of an air conditioner, and slightly moaning when she exhaled. I almost laughed and rolled my eyes. Almost.

Instead, I dug my heels into the soft rug, closed my eyes, and flexed my fingers open. I tried to breathe, and moan, and wail a little, too. I let myself think about my dad, and then I remembered I wasn't supposed to be thinking but feeling within my body. I wondered if trying not to think is a thought as well.

I remembered when I was at my father's funeral and couldn't cry. I was all cried out.

I tuned into my chest, my gut, my shoulders. "What does your body say?" my therapist asked. I breathed in, and then I let out a scream, surprising myself, and her, as well as possibly her neighbours. My scream was low-pitched, hungry, guttural, locked somewhere deep inside. Now it was released.

As months passed, I watched the seasons transition. Cotton-candy pink cherry blossoms grew on the previously dead, bare trees. With the help of a patella brace, my chronic knee pain softened to a dull throb. I went for walks, getting lost in thought, coming up with new angles to old story ideas and edits for stagnant articles. Why was I the most creative when doing something else, removing myself from the elements of my home office and boxy laptop? Productivity seems to be the antithesis of creativity, but so often we try to stick them in an unhappy relationship. How can you find room for innovation and failure when you're following a rigid plan? We push ourselves to schedule time for achieving our goals, and then we feel frustrated when we realize we can only get the desired outcome by letting go of control.

My best thoughts always showed up in the shower, when the hot water ran across my skin and slipped down the drain. As I squeezed shaving cream into my palm and lathered my bare legs, ideas popped up. Of course, I couldn't write them down, so I repeated them to myself, formulating, drafting stories in my head. I tried to hold on to them, but when I turned off the water, they started to fade away, slipping down the drain with the suds.

Sometimes I thought about that snowboarding jump. How free I felt flying through the air over a small, icy hump, before my body betrayed me and the mountains reminded me of my own fragility. How drastically my life has changed since. When I recalled falling, my back ached and stiffened like a wooden plank. The memories were stored deep in my muscles; the trauma etched into my splintered bones. Sometimes, I kissed my knees, grateful they still worked. Other times, I resented my body, especially new injuries like the knee pain that kept holding me back.

Sometimes I thought about my dad. How he would braid my hair before a dance recital because my mom's hands weren't strong enough to pull the strands tight. How he drove my high school basketball bus to tournaments around Alberta, cheering in the stands while I fumbled the ball into the hoop. These images of my tall, salt-and-pepper-haired father with his friendly grin and teddy bear disposition tugged on my heart like an anchor. Sometimes, the grief began to drown me. Other times, I floated, feeling happy to have a good dad to miss at all.

I fidgeted in my seat as I waited for what I hoped would be my final physiotherapy appointment. When called, I stood up and placed my full weight on my left knee.

"It's feeling so much better," I gushed to my physiotherapist as she led me into the room. "Not one hundred percent, but maybe eighty."

"That's great!" she said. "Have you been jogging?"

I squinted at her, wondering why everyone wanted us to run right after we could walk. "No," I admitted. "But there's something else I want to work on before I get there." My fingers travelled to the scars on my spine as I finally felt ready to tell her my full story.

"Wow," she said. "Sure, we can work on that."

Armed with new exercises, I exited the building with my head up. Working on my knee and spine and body and soul wasn't a time-bound problem. There was no simple solution or three-step plan for rehabbing my joints and understanding my emotions. I'd have to keep bettering them—bettering myself—forever, getting knocked down, standing back up, and pushing forward again.

Maybe that was the point.

On Father's Day the following year, Tavis and I drove out to a park near the airport. We sat at a picnic table while the wind ruffled the green leaves around us. He started by asking me what my dad was like. I talked about his love of motorcycles and sports cars, memories of us camping together, and how proud he'd be that I was following my dream of being a travel writer. The tears came quick, and they fell often.

We spent an hour in that open field, squinting in the harsh sunshine and bracing against the breeze that swept my tears away. Talking about my dad, letting my raw emotions show in front of others, wasn't something I'd anticipated when I began this journey, but it was exactly what I needed.

When we finally packed up and left the picnic table, I was struck with a sad thought: As cathartic as it was to openly tell stories and share memories of my dad, he was still dead. Nothing would change the fact that I would never create new memories with him. I was caught in a loop, where I'd have to continue doing this, facing my fears and my trauma, year after year. But I also felt a little surge of pride, hope, and love for that twenty-year-old girl with a back full of metal and a hopeless heart, too scared to face her overwhelming emotions.

Therapy wasn't linear like I'd wanted. I had to let my plan of getting better ebb and flow, without concentrating too much on the end. There was no end. My grief would be with me forever. So would my body, and all the aches, pains, and annoyances that accompany being human and growing older. How lucky, I thought, just to be.

Before another therapy appointment that August, I decided it would be my last session. As the date approached, I began feeling anxious and uncertain. Why did I feel the need to "finish" by now?

I realized that the deadlines I set upon myself were just that: my deadlines. No one expected me to be over my dad's death, to have my memoir published as a bestseller, or to heal my body enough to hike, snowboard, or run like I used to. I was the only one expecting such lofty goals, and by chastising myself for not meeting them, I wasn't giving myself enough credit for trying. For growing. For just being.

I knocked on my therapist's door, and I let go. Of my checklist. Of my plan. Of my need to be over and done or better and normal. I began to accept I'd always need some form of therapy for the rest of my life: physical, mental, emotional. And that's okay. It's human. It's me.

It turns out productivity is a lot more like creativity than I thought. Rather than a delineated checklist, it's a brainstorming bubble bouncing back and forth. I'm a work in progress that will continue changing, growing, and healing as long as I keep breathing. We're all messy first drafts with endless opportunities for edits. There is no straight and narrow path to completion; productivity and creativity need each other. Both require patience, openness, flexibility, and just showing up, again and again.

On a stunning, blue-bird Wednesday, I stepped into my therapist's little sanctuary. She closed the heavy door and led me into her living room. I made myself comfortable among the fluffy pillows on the beige couch, the glass table resting on the soft rug, the familiar box of tissues to catch my tears when they fell.

Once again, I was ready to heal.

ALISON KARLENE HODGINS is an award-winning travel writer and editor based in Vancouver, British Columbia. She's travelled to over thirty-five different countries and has a Writing and Publishing diploma, a Bachelor of Journalism degree, and an MFA in Creative Nonfiction. Her work has appeared in the Globe and Mail, the Huffington Post, Fodor's, explore, and CBC. Alison is writing her debut memoir about breaking her back while snowboarding in the French Alps. Follow her adventures at aroundtheworldwithalison.com.

Writing as an ADHDer!

I will begin by telling you the story of a working-class, neurodivergent mother, PhD graduate, university lecturer and researcher, peer reviewer, and author. I do not have the background of an average academic; I was a school dropout at fifteen. I have always been a creative individual with a love of writing, but with undiagnosed ADHD (until recently), I have always struggled with writing.

I was born and bred a Yorkshire lass in Leeds, England, moving to a rural village called Ballygar in Galway, Ireland, before my teen years. I did well at school in Leeds, the teaching methods worked for me, being diverse, creative, and collaborative.

"Jess, I love your story about Peanut Butter Girl." Mr. Mercer smiled as he held my makeshift book in his hands.

"Thanks, Mr. Mercer. I loved writing this," I replied.

"I think you should put this in for the under eleven's short story writing competition, and how about you read it at circle time today?" he said, handing me back my story.

Mr. Mercer always supported my writing.

But then I found myself in Ballygar village, at a school opposite in every way. The teaching methods were focused on discipline and learning alone from textbooks. Many subjects like Irish history were completely new to me, so I fell behind before I even started, and I did not know a word of the Irish language.

I remember sitting in the back of an Irish class one day. Mrs. Doyle shouted at me in Gaelic, I had no idea what she was saying. She made me write the homework off the blackboard, which was impossible to complete when I did not know the language. I put it to the back of my mind. Instead, I was excited about English class, my favourite subject.

"I want you to turn to page nine in your poetry book and learn the poem off by heart," Mrs. Kelly ordered.

"How are we supposed to learn all of this?" I whispered to Mary, who sat beside me.

"Ciúnas! *Ciúnas,* I said!" Mrs. Kelly shouted an Irish word that meant quietness.

I felt a block come up. I could not learn like this. I would zone out. During each class, teachers quizzed me about homework or in-class activities that I could not complete. I would often be thrown out of class for non-compliance. The teachers did not care that I did not understand. I eventually started skipping class. After long-term detentions and thousands of "I will not [insert wrong-doing here]" lines, I finally got expelled from the class I needed for university. Not one single teacher seemed to believe in me. It was then that I decided to drop out.

It took eight years for me to make it to university; however, when I did, I loved the learning experience, which was very different from high school. Although it came with its challenges, I found ways around them that worked for me. When I was coming to the end of my undergraduate degree, I realized how much I loved education and did not want to leave. This led me to a master's degree, and eventually a PhD.

In the second year of my PhD, my adviser voiced the concern that my writing may not be at a high enough standard; he was worried I may have dyslexia. This came from the very best place. I was struggling and I had been in denial, I just wanted this so much. Over the next year, I worked very hard and found strategies to prove us both wrong. The best thing you can say to someone with ADHD is "you can't do that!" Wait and see what happens next! Within a year, my committee told me that my academic writing was one of the best they had seen in over a year. Within two years, my adviser told me one of my chapters was the best he had ever seen from a student. I then began publishing academic manuscripts and became a reviewer for two international academic journals. It was at this point I found out that I did not have dyslexia, I have ADHD.

For those unaware of what adult attention deficit/hyperactivity disorder is—and, from experience, there are wide misconceptions of it—I will give a brief explanation. An individual with ADHD has challenges related to executive functioning. This means the individual can struggle with initiating tasks and focusing and sustaining their attention. They may have challenges with their working memory. Regulation can be an issue in many aspects—self-regulation of behaviours, emotional regulation, as well as regulating alertness, effort, and processing speed.[1] This can make daily life a very real struggle. One important thing to note is that it does not mean that there is a deficit of attention, as the name implies, not when the person is interested (this is called situational variability). For example, I struggle with basic household tasks, but I can hyper-focus on my research as I am interested in it. Individuals with ADHD also have many positive traits, too many to name here, but they include: creativity, intelligence, originality, empathy, justice warrior, fun, and risk-taking—definitely a person you would like to know.

With this knowledge, I started to learn about my strengths, how to use them in my best interest, and how to recognize and overcome the challenges that I faced. I would like to share some of the strategies that worked for me, in the hope that they will help others, whether they have ADHD or not.

All Those Somethings Add Up

Before I had my now six-year-old, my writing time was not limited. When I was not working, I would sit at a laptop for long periods. Even though I was not time-pressured, I got very little writing done. Reflecting back, I needed pressure, I needed to know I only had two hours of my son's nap time to write. Instead, I took my time, I procrastinated, I was easily persuaded to take coffee breaks, I would take on extra work tasks and do those instead, and my time was not productive.

After I had my son, writing time became a valued treasure. When I got it, I used it in the best way I could. This meant no procrastination, saying no to people who tried to take this precious time off me and physically writing it in my diary so nothing else took its place. As the saying goes, it takes thirty days to build a habit. I went to my home study every night at 8:00 PM to write after getting my son to bed, until I did it as naturally as drinking my morning coffee. Do I complain? Yes. I make a big cup of tea and, feeling sorry for myself, I drag myself up the stairs, open the study door, sit at my desk, and turn on my computer. Once I do this, it is never as bad. *It is just two hours, I can do this,* I internally chant.

Before losing all my writing time, I used to believe that I could only write in large blocks of time. I have now learned that I can grab my laptop during a work break and pop into the café on campus or slip into the library for that half-hour and write something. All those somethings add up. It never feels like a task when I know I only have such a short time, so I write as quickly as I can and before I know it, the time is over and a fresh paragraph stares back at me from the page. I view writing differently now, and writing is embedded into my daily life.

Starting With What I Love

People are always told to start with the task that they do not like, the one they find hard, and get it out of the way. Once this is done, they can focus on what they enjoy. Wrong! ADHDers are told to do the opposite. If they start with what they do not like or find challenging, they will be so bored or blocked they will never get past it. I start with what I am passionate about, the part of the work that does not feel like work, that ignites me, that fills me with so much joy that I do not want to stop! I always leave the boring or complex parts to the end. But because this is all I have left to do, and I am so close to the finish line, I am motivated to push through it.

However, sometimes even if I love what I am doing, I get writer's block. During the ADHD coaching training I undertook, I was introduced to the VIA (VIAcharacter.org),[3] which is a character strengths survey. I took a short test by answering questions relating to my personality, and the survey generated my personalized strengths profile, with my twenty-four top strengths. My main strengths, in order, are creativity, love of learning, teamwork, bravery, and social intelligence. Shortly after taking the VIA, I was working on an assessment for a postgraduate course. The brief was pages long, and I was getting lost in it. There were a lot of boxes to fill out, and I felt restricted. This is not a good feeling for ADHDers. I started to feel stressed and became blocked. So, I paused. I remembered the VIA. I asked myself, "What is my greatest strength?" Of course, creativity. I needed to be creative with this. I took the brief and flung it behind my shoulder to the floor. I grabbed a notebook and pencil and started drawing a diagram similar to a brainstorm with all of my ideas. I was feeling really excited at this stage! Within a very short space of time, I had devised a new model and had linked it to theory. I paused and drew on my greatest strength of creativity and made the assessment work for me, instead of trying to fit in those boxes of the assessment that were holding me back.

Taking Up a Book Obsession

My writing and grammar were so poor up until recently (due to ADHD), that when I read my work aloud during the redraft phase, I would realize I missed keywords from each sentence. I also poorly structured my ideas. Using a thesaurus to broaden my vocabulary, I soon learned I used the words out of context and did not understand them. I decided to accept my Yorkshire dialect and found my own style of writing that reflected my authentic self. I practised several strategies to improve.

One of these strategies was reading outside of the academic literature I read for university, mainly memoirs and fiction. I enjoy reading each night and weekend and have joined Goodreads for reading challenges. I joined two book clubs, where we meet once a month over Zoom. This is not only extremely enjoyable due to the social nature, but it keeps me motivated to read, and discussing the texts adds another layer of learning.

If you are looking for me and I am not writing, I am usually in a bookstore, library, or thrift store searching for my next read, or in my home study or a local café with a coffee and a book. I have way too many books in my home library for the time I have to read, and I know the postman curses me for having to call to my house almost daily with second-hand buys or books from the swap group I joined on Facebook. But looking through my shelves at the worn covers, anticipating the fantasy I will enter next, and deciding what to read excites me, while also helping to passively improve my writing skills. Shortly after this book obsession, I realized that when I was writing, new words were automatically flowing from my fingertips to the keyboard and onto the page. I began to doubt myself and would Google the meaning of these words. They were always correct. All this reading was widening my vocabulary without me knowing, in such a fun way.

Not Crying When Reading Philosophy Books

In the first few years of my PhD and prior, I struggled with academic reading. I would read a chapter and realize I had not processed one single idea. This processing issue is very much related to ADHD, but something most readers can connect to when reading something uninteresting or complex. I needed to find ways to beat this. I remember one day reading a philosophy book and crying out of frustration because I could not get a grasp on it. I then looked up research articles where the authors had written about the philosopher's ideas after applying them in their own studies; this gave me a better understanding of what they meant. I then went back to the original text and read aloud. I would pace up and down the room reading the words like an actor practising her script the night before her leading role, or sitting on my leather chair I swung in sync to the words like music. For me, it was movement and multiple levels of processing, reading, and hearing the words. If I saw an idea that was interesting to me, I would underline it in pencil and take notes in the margins, then go to my manuscript and immediately write down any rough ideas I had for redrafting at a later date. I spent time going back and forth between the paragraphs and the manuscript; it was a slow process, but it felt like such an achievement to understand these philosophical texts and to rewrite them with my own reflections, in an understandable dialogue.

Reigniting My Writing World

If something is boring, ADHDers are asked how they can reignite it. Interest yields hyper-focus and productivity, but disinterest causes procrastination and a lack of intended results. I have reignited my environment for writing in many ways.

Pre-pandemic, I reignited by writing on the train, in a café, or a library. During the pandemic, like most, I was forced to work from home. I used my creative vision and converted the spare room into a home study. It is a warm, cozy room that smells of old, worn, musty books, brewed coffee, and burning candles with strong aromas. This was my space to read, write, and drink coffee to my heart's content. I had reignited my writing world, and I never wanted to leave my home study again.

I have always been interested in technology. I somehow stumbled across a Facebook group for writers who used distraction-free writing tools. One of these was an Alphasmart Neo—a word processor from the 1990s. I was so intrigued by them that I went onto eBay and started bidding. They are not expensive, but among collectors, they are well-sought-after retro machines. The machine is solely for typing and meant for first drafts; this method of working was not only distraction-free, but it reignited the experience. I then learned about modern distraction-free writing tools made by a company called Astrohaus. Sometime later, I received a gift of a Freewrite and, as time went on, I treated myself to a Freewrite Traveler. I now had a collection of distraction-free writing tools, so I could swap between them to keep things fresh. I love them all for different reasons. The Alphasmart Neo for its retro feel: the words flow off your fingertips and onto a small screen that lights up in the dark, and the batteries will last over a year without replacement. The Freewrite looks beautiful, the rugged aluminum body is the closest to a typewriter, and the sound of the mechanical keyboard puts me into a writing trance as the paper-like e-ink screen fills with words. My favourite of all is the Freewrite Traveler, which I can bring anywhere. It's the size and weight of a small notepad but much quieter for travelling with its scissor switch keyboard. Constantly reigniting my process helps me to constantly write.

Finding a Supportive Writing Mentor

During my PhD studies, I joined a PhD writing group at the campus where I worked. We met for regular writing boot camps, where there was a mentor available to give feedback on samples of our writing. My mentor had no background in my area of expertise, but he specialized in writing. Each session, we met over coffee, and he taught me something new about the craft. His advice was invaluable. Very soon after this began, my PhD advisers started to notice a huge improvement in my writing; my confidence grew, and I began to publish.

Immersing Myself in Writing

The PhD writing group was more than just a space to write; we supported each other in our struggles as writers. I've attended other writing events with the group, my favourite so far being a writing retreat where I could concentrate on writing without the distractions of work and family. I also participated in academic writing classes and shut-up-and-write sessions, which basically use the Pomodoro technique[3]: the group talks for five minutes, then shuts up and writes for twenty-five, followed by five more minutes of talk, followed by more writing. We also held events, where we presented our research to each other for peer feedback.

All these experiences are supportive, enjoyable ones that took me away from the isolation that often comes with research and writing. When my confidence in academic writing grew, I decided to brave my lifelong dream to be a creative writer and aimed to publish a memoir. I joined an online memoir class, and when it was complete, one of the students and I decided to continue to meet weekly, use the Pomodoro technique, and read each other's work for feedback. I then took more creative writing classes. Following this, I joined an online writer's platform called the London Writers' Salon, where I could access recordings of sessions on the writing craft and attend live Zoom writing hours with writers all over the world. On top of learning so much about writing craft, there was no way I *couldn't* write when I immersed myself in it!

Visualization

My final strategy is visualization. I remember pacing up and down my research office before my first lecturer position interview. My hands were sweating, my breathing fast, and I was overwhelmed. *What am I doing? I am not good enough to get this job.* Then I turned my thinking around: *Yes, I am.* I remembered why I was applying for the job and visualized myself getting it. Right now, I am visualizing holding the book with this chapter in my hands. I am visualizing seeing it on a bookshelf in my local bookshop. I am visualizing you reading it. Whenever I want something that I believe is out of reach, I close my eyes tight, and I visualize myself doing or having it. I got that lecturer job, and all the other things I visualized. If I can see myself doing the desired activity, there are fewer mental blocks in my way. There is a higher chance that I will meet that goal because I see it as realistic. I believe in myself.

Final Thoughts

None of this is easy. It requires discipline, commitment, and motivation. But I love to write, and I have publishing goals, so that makes it easier. It has also become easier as I've received positive feedback on my writing and managed to publish—all motivators. It is still a challenge, with ADHD, work, research, and a child, but I have managed to make writing a part of my daily life.

I also do not want to downplay the challenges of ADHD. It can be very hard, and for some more so than others. I have been very lucky in being able to overcome many of the challenges, but I've trained in ADHD coaching, I've had my own ADHD coach to help me, and the character traits I personally possess for ADHD, such as hyperfocus and the passion to use my work for social change, have given me this drive. I hope you will source some inspiration from my story. Apart from my love of writing, the biggest motivator here is that I believe in myself as a writer.

DR. JESS MANNION is a mother, lecturer, researcher, peer reviewer, and author living in the UK. She prides herself on being a working-class, neurodivergent academic. Jess is a Health and Social Care Lecturer. Her research specializes in collaborative intellectual disability research on relationships and sexuality, using visual and creative research methods. She is based at Manchester Metropolitan University, UK. Jess has published academic writing and has a memoir in progress.

More Like a Garden

The first time I planted bulbs I did it all wrong. I covered each one, alone. Singly in a hole, alone. I dug a small tomb and then covered it with dirt. When spring came, there they were, lone shoots all over the yard, no symmetry. No intimacy. No cluster. A tulip here and there, a yellow narcissus with a gap and then a scrawny blue muscari, a single orange crocus. Grassy patches in between. The smallest hope popping up out of the sod. This is no way to plant a garden. What did I know? I was constantly fending for myself. I hated to need. Didn't understand togetherness or solitude. We bury people alone in graves. Next to each other, yet alone. I thought it was this way for flowers too. It's not and we ought to learn something from them, the way they gather and hold each other close. The way they are, next to one another. The layers. The difference. The inter-being. The way they don't need tombs.

My answer isn't a straight line when asked how I became a florist. The path wasn't plotted; it was a squiggle I meandered along. I didn't want to design for weddings or, as I like to call it, *the wedding machine,* where the work often took me. I wanted to be holed up in a light-filled studio for hours with flowers for company, their muddy scent against the dry spine of a notebook. The spark began in my mother's garden with hummingbirds buzzing above a rowan tree, their wings moving so fast they were invisible. There, I tasted the sour stalks of rhubarb, inhaled the intoxicating scent of lilacs, and held soft worms in my soiled hands. Digging around in the dirt beside Mum, finding weedy roots to pluck, happily helping. So when I finally had green space of my own, in my first Toronto flat, I decided to give growing a try. As a novice gardener I was stunned the bulbs and seeds I planted came up at all. That simply being willing to start was enough. Care came later.

My life was transient for a long time, but gardens made me feel rooted. I planted one wherever I ended up. Even when renting derelict ground. The resting fallow periods scared me the most though. All that darkness, the quiet within the soil seemingly doing nothing, was uncomfortable. Frozen ground mixed with browning leaves reminded me of death, or worse, loneliness. As an artistic person fallow ground was akin to self-doubt and creative droughts. All of which I resisted welcoming. I didn't understand it was nourishment.

My friend said she entered Dia Chelsea, and the room smelled of cinnamon and clove. A penetrable aroma. An earth-lined room. All the sculptures in the exhibit were soil compositions. One from floor to ceiling, a monolith structure titled *El abrazo* (*The Embrace*, 2023). My friend witnessed Delcy Morelos, a Colombian artist who has employed earth as her primary material for over a decade. Through her multisensory art, Morelos invites guests to touch the soil mounds: *Earth is as fragile as we are.* These large sculptures were made to mimic peat, a healing fuel. Morelos disrupts sensory hierarchies of sight, evoking smell and feel. She aims to unlock creative and spiritual power through colour, geometry, and the land—understands land as a symbol of conflict, an obsession triggering inequality, and yet she turns the pure raw matter over and looks at it with reverence. In an installation series titled *Eva*, the soil is red from iron, just as the blood in our veins is red from iron. Morelos says humans have a deep relation to the earth, but we have lost our awareness of it, of the cycles of life, death, and rebirth. She says, "To be in touch with the earth and to enter within it is to be in touch with what constitutes and nourishes us; the bedrock where life develops while it is inhabited by the soul."[1]

I didn't always know I would be a writer.

What I did know was I would make things.

As a kid I performed plays with my sister, made up songs on a tape recorder, painted and stapled my own books. I was a hungry girl. A wanting person. Since writing allowed for continuous learning, to make almost anything through words, to create worlds and emotional responses, I chose it. A wilful spirit. Though I excelled at math and science, it took me years to realize just because I was good at something didn't mean it should be my life's work. Excelling and desiring are very different qualities.

Twenty was when I began writing regularly in a notebook. Stacks sit under my desk as I type. I slept on a couch then, paying rent at an apartment nicknamed *518 Jane where life is the party*. Working as a receptionist in Rexdale by day, noodling on my guitar in off hours, I tried to pen my thoughts. The notebooks have a fancy name now that I have an MFA—archives. The notebooks contain the kind of writing I don't want anyone to read. This was before I knew what prosody and syntax were. Before poetics.

Journaling began purely as an expression—to see what I thought, notice my moods, and order my life. I was good at stuffing my feelings down. I only cried when surprised by something more beautiful than I expected. Writing gave me language for my interior world.

Though these journals sprawl, ramble, and are illegible at times, there are breaks when light, shimmery prose swells up. Or some brief, blunt line comes out just right. I see where I learned to name things: shrubs, trees, birds, and flowers. An unusual turn of phrase surprises me. This is why I write.

Writing didn't happen all at once. It took time to find my voice outside academia and cultivate *my* thoughts so something meaningful could grow. To distinguish between weedy bits and veracity, to let go of jargon for straightforwardness, to set aside ego, which isn't always easy, for the wellness of spirit, something true to self.

In my twenties, I had a few breakdowns. Terror alchemized sleepless nights. Loss of appetite and relentless bouts of anxiety. Insomnia befriended me when I left home to study at the University of Waterloo. A disappearing sensation visited while I studied there. As a major in geochemistry, I pored over books learning about rock formations and chemical elements that make up our geological systems. I studied strata lines in a lab. I wore safety goggles and used a microscope. I took notes and didn't realize I was searching for existential answers. I liked expanding my mind in this way, but the disappearing sensation increased with the weight of my work and the loneliness I felt. I tried to make friends, smoked hookah in dorms while studying for finals. I went to parties in the next college over. I bought *O* by Damien Rice in the HMV and played the CD on repeat. Turns out sad songs didn't help. I stayed out all night and ate breakfast with strangers, but nothing distracted me from the disappearing.

Tired and unresponsive, on the bottom bunk of a shared dorm, wearing the same clothes I'd been in for days; that's how Mum found me. I didn't know how to balance life and school, didn't know how to talk about myself, or even recognize what was happening. Mum helped me pack up my belongings, which all fit inside a suitcase. I dropped out and took a job waitressing, learned about ice wine, table settings, and how to fold a napkin. I was getting "right cultured," as Dad joked. I got a membership at the YMCA. Practised yoga before it was cool. The gym wasn't fancy, but I learned deep breathing and sat in the steam room until I was a prune.

Soon, I switched my undergrad to York University to be near my high school boyfriend. A mistake. Add it to the compost heap. The breakdowns took me into a vortex where reality and dream were interchangeable, time and daylight unknowable. I thought I had completely lost my mind. Embarrassed, I wondered if I would ever return to myself. A chemistry professor wrote a concerned email about not attending an exam when my grades were so high. I read it, thought it was kind and wrote back, "I'm not returning to class."

The breakings isolated me and became something I didn't discuss because I thought it wasn't normal. When my high school boyfriend asked me to move in with him, I said yes despite the nagging in my stomach.

Not once after I had these breakings did I rest. I treated them like a cold and went headlong into something else the minute I regained strength. This was necessary then because I was afraid of being swallowed up by emotions, too feeling—sensitive woman.

Telling a story straight is not easy. There are too many layers, like soil—bedrock, weathered fragments, subsoil, topsoil, organic matter—too many versions of self to turn over and show what's actually happening on the surface.

I floundered through my twenties and my journals piled up in a Rubbermaid bin. They remind me I'm a writer on days when

I can't find words. Pages written for myself became how I handled the myriad of moods that swirled inside over—relationships in contemporary life, self-care, balancing making money with making art, marrying or not, having children or not, helping aging parents, keeping a home, keeping a lover, returning to school, and growing a career. In my writing I see all the variations of a self, the good and the ugly. All that breaks down and becomes the soil of a life.

Turns out, maintaining mental well-being in a mind-fuck of a world isn't so common after all. A friend said, in one of her sorrow seasons, she felt like no one wanted to be near her, that her loss was too much, and people could sense her sadness. I piped up, "People don't like to be around grief. It reminds them of their vulnerability and our inevitable mortality." I thought of university, all the house parties I'd been to and how no one ever talked about their fears. There were bongs and chugging and bushfires that burned into the sky. There was kissing and burnt toast and lovers fighting. There was always a boy who looked safe and beautiful, like a folk singer who might become my true love. There was me in a room hiding the breakings. Then I thought of my fear, of the resting fallow periods and why I began to teach myself about flowers.

I became interested in the names of flowers in the winter of 2014. I'd moved with my then-husband to a redbrick home in central Hamilton. The backyard had a garden, but I could hardly wait through the cold months to see what would grow. While the ground was frozen, I read Constance Spry's *The Art of Arranging Flowers*, went to the snobby florist's shop to buy stems each week, placed them in bud vases to study their form—*craspedia, freesia, ranunculus, astrantia*. I noted the names in my journal, began to learn, forgetting myself in the best of ways. It was an education in seeing, where the most intricate ordinary world became known, detailed. Observation helped me learn to follow a sentence intuitively.

After years of this practice, my words stopped being hyper-critical and "became more and more a mere description of what I was doing and the things I saw," as George Orwell put it in *Why I Write*.[2] As I noticed, slowly, what my thoughts were, I let out all I could on the blank page. I observed my disquiet and began inquiry. Questions like "Why write, why art?" or "Does beauty matter?" I saw where I held back with silences between words. I felt the gentleness of a semicolon and the knife of a dash. I let my observations form in playful, embodied ways, crushing solidago between my fingers, the cottony tufts of clematis seed, the stink of skunk cabbage, and the golden green ball of dried Queen Anne's lace, each floret made of hundreds of flowers, how they smell of carrots.

Towards the end of my twenties, my marriage began decomposing. Soon, I found myself working in the wedding industry, while going through a divorce. I reflexed tulips and tears fell. I went to therapy. Nothing could have prepared me for such a stark contrast of reality.

"I can't be a writer," I said, brushing my fingers over the sleeve of my sweater. Silence hung like a fog. "I'm not doing enough. My desk is covered with unread books. Writing gets done in fractured hours." I sniffled. "Plus, I'll be poor forever. If I commit to writing, to being an artist—I'll be poor."

My therapist nodded, took a sip of her tea. "What's your definition of success?"

The air from my mouth was warm. I wanted to yell at her that this had nothing to do with what I was saying. I wanted to say *you're not even listening.*

She let the quiet linger, then, "play is productive." That's what she said. And when I heard this, my mind rejected it, like a tape that wouldn't work. I was a full-time florist in a seven-billion-dollar industry, I had clients, freelanced, worked contracts, farmed and sold flowers at stands, and even though I'd never planned for this, I was surviving. There was no time for play. Surviving was all I knew how to do then.

Writing this essay, I reread *The Getaway Car* by Ann Patchett,[3] hoping it would spark something. It did, but it also left me slightly despondent. My life is so far from Patchett's. While I read, I discovered she wrote her first novel at twenty-nine. I wanted to know how much time there was between her success and the moment she called "a dark day of waitressing." I've had many dark days of waitressing. Before my acceptance into an MFA program, I bartended at a restaurant where cockroaches and sexual harassment were the norm. I wrote in the mornings and then went to work, sometimes until 2:00 or 4:00 AM. I promised myself I would work on my craft between shifts and kept that vow—no matter the cost.

That same year, 2019, I audited English Lit classes at McMaster on the side while slinging dishes and mixing drinks. I wanted the freedom to return to part of myself that would have chosen English and Art History as a major in undergrad. There was a freedom to studying poetry and the novel for fun. I read Chopin's *Awakening*, Zora Neale Hurston's *Their Eyes Were Watching God*, and lingered over Emily Dickinson's *Wild Nights*. I bought used copies of the syllabus from The Printed Word and talked to the owner about narrative, hating traditional story forms and then loving them, how Hurston's dialect paced my reading differently. My copies had the pencil markings of those who'd read the books before me. Broken book spines meant more to me than a new copy.

I read Cheever for the first time and Carver again. I read Sylvia Plath's *Ariel*, not because it was on the list, but because I wanted to. I read Thoreau and Whitman, compared their different perspectives on the natural world, one a stripped-down life, the other one of multitudes. I read Adrienne Rich's *Diving Into The Wreck* at the professor's recommendation and found solace for the girl who studied geochemistry and knew the words are purposes, the words are maps. We read poems out loud and discussed them. We wrote stories and listened in. We gave feedback and emphasized the importance of slow reading. I wasn't there to get credits, so I didn't worry about performance or the merit of a grade. The desire was for myself alone and that felt pure. I studied the texts out of curiosity. My marriage was over, but I was in love, my mind buzzing over literature. I was playing.

I think about those scattered bulbs in my first garden and how they still provided pollen for bees and some of those bees kept warm and alive in a hive through winter. How everything is connected even if it isn't beautiful. That soil can't exist without decay, compost is partly shit, and yet life can't exist without the soil. Comparing myself to a revered writer, like Ann Patchett, is a bad habit, but turning the habit around to compare myself to where I've been takes me somewhere new. I stopped looking at my first drafts and contrasting them against final drafts of published authors. I took the writers I loved and made them part of my soil.

The lessons Patchett learned from her writing teachers become my lessons, there's a cyclical rhythm. Grace Paley's teaching folds in like mulch when Patchett writes:

> She taught me that writing must not be compartmentalized. You don't step out of the stream of your life to do your work . . . work was the life, and who you were as mother, teacher, friend, citizen, activist, and artist was all the same person . . . I can teach you how to write a better sentence, how to write dialogue, maybe even how to construct a plot. But I can't teach you how to have something to say.[4]

I wrote this down and then looked up more essays on writing I'd dogeared.

While I indulged in self-consciousness, I found conflicting methods. Then something wonderful happened: I realized by reading other writers I was again putting off finding my own words for things. There's nothing that prepares an artist more than discovering *their* creative process. Being too awed or intimidated by success can prevent a new writer from finding their own way. Regardless of the artistic medium, mastery is to enter in and practise.

Morelos understands the difference between seeing and entering. She doesn't want her art to be viewed, she wants it to be experienced. She dissolves boundaries between soil and water, making mud. She uses mud to paint ceramics and point out that death fertilizes life. I don't want my words to be seen. I want them to be entered.

I do not feel qualified to write this, and yet that's precisely the place I've tried to write from—the underground. The compost pile where everything rots and breaks down, then after a long period of darkness, there's life—some gorgeous green sprouting in an unlikely season.

I folded my floristry business to write regularly. It was an artistic leap, which was exhilarating and terrifying at once.

The risk of shifting one artistic medium for another was difficult. I had to believe in the initial wild leap, the uncanny idea that I could be a writer. I was tired of running my floristry business, of farming, teaching, freelancing, and designing, all while working other contract jobs. Between work, I attended literary events, writing workshops, and poetry readings, telling myself once my business was sustainable, then I'd devote myself to the craft. To leave my thoughts in bins under my desk began to feel like soil prepped and neglected. Something gone hard, dry. Seedlings left in a tray. An abundance of potted shrubs waiting for the earth, unable to grow larger than their pots, nowhere to roam. I longed to devote myself to writing but to begin anew I'd need rest, to lay fallow from other artistic pursuits.

Almost a decade after my ugly lone bulb planting, I had soil, compost, and mulch delivered to my home. This is the kind of thing people do when they own a home. It doesn't matter that I am no longer a homeowner. I have planted a garden in every place I've rented. On a scorching summer day, mid-August, sweat above my lip, I began sheet-mulching the front lawn. I'd never had a front garden and the idea of people walking by to admire borage or calendula spilling from the stone edge was rewarding enough.

The big mesh bags of dirt were an eyesore, but I thought, *soon the flowers.* Violet throats of iris rising. Cobalt cornflowers. Red tulip mouths. Checkered frits. All of them, tiny potentials. Possibilities opening. Nectar for insects. A place larger than a sonnet.

In an interview with Sheila Heti in *The Creative Independent*, Thora Siemsen asked: "How do you account for the interruptions of your social calendar while writing a book?"

"I don't consider it interruptions. It took me seven years to write *Motherhood* so I don't consider it an interruption. I need life in my life."[5]

Writing material isn't only when I've treated art in a serious way. It's also all the years leading up to sitting at my desk and the interruptions. The scrappy, hungry years of juggling work and fitting writing in where I could, was the work. Playing was the work. Maybe I was bad at writing, but at least I was writing, not just talking about writing. As a gardener I've spent years digging, splitting, potting, tucking. With each move I've transplanted my garden, dividing the roots, giving some to friends and leaving some for new tenants to enjoy. My canvases have been grass, clover, and weeds.

This time I sheet mulched. My own land-art project. I tore pages from stacks of the *New York Review of Books* (NYRB), spreading dirt out evenly with a rake to hold the loose paper down. As I layered newsprint one on top of the other, I noticed headlines from the year: *Another New World, Lovesick for a God, The Roots of Our Madness. Learning to Grieve. The Right to Belong.* Almost two decades after the breakings and we're still highlighting the same themes. I watered the bare soil for weeks, waiting for it to decompose, for the recycled words of last year to become home for seeds and new roots.

Upon entering, the room is dimly lit and Morelos's exhibit, *Cielo terrenal* (Earthly Heaven), looks as if you're staring into a void. The dark gallery is silent and lightless, but the smell of cinnamon and cloves are the offering. Her art is black, monochrome, just as a bed of soil looks. She says you don't go up into the heavens when you die, you go down here, to dust of the earth, where you transform into other forms of life.

I hadn't had time to read the articles in the NYRBs, my attention split as I worked on my first manuscript. Like many, the uncertainty of the pandemic clouded my mind. I was distracted and unemployed. I was either writing the book or reading and thinking about the book. Then I was working too many jobs, oscillating between four part-time gigs. Endurance and agony were the two constants. Like any decent art, the aim was to finish.

The fallow periods became part of the process. Distance from the work. An acceptance of the subtle stillness making room for growth. I left the soil patch on the front yard for months and stared at the black earth when I arrived home. Nothing but uneven ground to welcome me. For once, I didn't think *my brain is broken*. I told myself the self-doubt and creative droughts meant something even if the only meaning was flowers. I demanded proof from these ugly qualities in the dark while waiting. I paid attention, persisted despite them, and the day finally came when they began to grow my life instead of destroying it.

Claiming I was a writer happened after I began sharing, reading, and submitting work. I pruned, weeded, and learned to sculpt the arrangements of words. Not only the order of words, but sounds, associations, details, and voice, everything said and not said and the spaces between. The writing and not writing—patient work beneath the work. The piles of journals no one will read, notes in the margins of books, newsprint under the soil, the tender hand guiding a seedling toward a trellis, sitting beside a mother on a gurney, helping a sister move. Knowing art is a generous act of emotional labour, a series of unnoticeable acts with fallow and fruitful seasons. With compost heaps and broken ground. With sowing, waiting, and darkness. Germination, rest, and yields.

I have found, as an artist, I work more like a garden, less like a machine.

Morelos's *El abrazo* (The Embrace), overcomes the senses. A powerful, towering piece where something small is made large. A reminder that we are nature too.

My new garden is a mass collage of print, soil, and sweat, a living painting plastered with dirt instead of oils or acrylic. One neighbour stops over to give me a bottle of water. "Incredible," he says, shaking his head. I think of Natalia Ginzburg's words: "We are deeply, painfully rooted in every being and thing in the world."[6] A mix of thoughts and images, conversations and silences, good and bad art, all caught up in the compost heap to make something new.

Soon green beyond language will form in this front yard.

Seeds will split and crack in muddy months, growing into flowers, some for cutting and giving to friends, some to sit in vessels on my table, and some destined to wilt on the vine, sowing themselves for next year

Later, the lawn is browned with cedar mulch. The squirrels scatter their nuts as I smooth it over with the rake, so the neighbours won't mind the lumpy brown sight. The sod is soft enough to plant. I sweep the muck built up on the sidewalk after rainfall. The transplants are waiting to be tucked into place. I dig holes and plant a bundle of tulip bulbs, a cluster of double daffodils, a handful of fritillaria, muscari, crocus, so they'll grow beside one another. I know to plant narcissus close to tulips now to keep rodents away. I plant lily of the valley. I plant sage and acidanthera. I go out and weed between writing, let rest, let dirt under my fingernails, let witnessing life outside myself. I stop worrying now about why I'm doing this or that. I think, *I need more money*, and let that pass through. My hands are full of soil, and I think of the promise of what will be, all that's unseen. I feel part of something larger than self. Flower friends gift plants back to me. They split their abundance—monarda, prairie smoke, mountain mint, northern sea oats, sweetgrass, and rudbeckia triloba. I line a path with stones, rounded rock buried halfway in the earth so when I walk along it, barefoot in summer, I will feel warmth against my soles. Sun and stone and skin. I'm not going away from life now, not shutting down to escape the empty abyss, not disappearing from the discomfort. Now, I'm sitting in the dirt, on the front lawn, cultivating a life that might allow for the next creation.

JESSICA PAYNE is a writer, poet, and interdisciplinary artist at work on a book. Her work has been featured in the *Hamilton Spectator, Green Living Magazine, Urbanicity, Flower House Detroit,* and elsewhere. Previously, she was founder and creative director of an ecological design studio. Her botanical art was recognized throughout Canada, the US, and Mexico. She's the recipient of HA&L Short Works Prize in literary nonfiction, and her poetry was published in the 2023 Contact Photography Festival and the 2022 Wayzgoose Anthology. She lives in Toronto with her partner, rescue cat, and beloved garden.

A Regulating Home

My tea mug is sitting on my desk. It's a beautiful mug, big and round with thick sides to keep the heat in. I finished my tea an hour ago. I should take the mug to the kitchen. If I take it to the kitchen, I should really wash it. The sink is full of dishes. I'll have to wash some of those before I can wash my mug. All that washing will take too long. I'll take the mug up to the kitchen later. After I've done some writing.

I write a few sentences. My eyes wander to my twisted sheets and sprawled comforter. I didn't make my bed this morning. Maybe I should make it now. Maybe I should hang up my night-gown. Maybe I should go through the stack of books next to my bed and put away the ones I'm not realistically going to read any time soon. Some of those are library books. I should check to see when they're due. I pick up my phone. Ten minutes later, I have renewed my books and put holds on several more. I look up from my phone and remember that I was writing.

I love to write. It's important to me, and, I think, good for me, in the way that a thing can feel torturous but relieve restlessness in the soul. Somehow, though, there always seems to be something more pressing to do. And even when I sit down to write, I am distracted. My most productive writing time is generally in cafés, guest rooms, and parks, where there are only so many tasks I can take responsibility for.

I have tried so many systems and tricks to get myself to write. I have used reminders and schedules and apps that locked my phone. I have tried sheer force of will. I have gradually increased the amount of time I spend writing, but by so little it doesn't feel like a victory. I was never able to write seriously, despite good intentions and productivity tips and a deep, nauseating desire, until I was diagnosed with autism.

It is still a badge of feminine success to have a spotless, beautiful home. Regardless of academic or professional accomplishments, regardless of creative pursuits or other obligations, women are expected to keep their homes well. To fail to have a well-kept home is not just a practical failure but a moral one. I feel the shame of it deeply.

When women visit one another for the first time, they shower compliments on the pristine, elegantly arranged homes. The homes that are basically clean and tidy escape with no comment. Homes that are messy or dirty receive the soul-crushing looks. Eyes fall on the mounds of possessions cluttering tables, or the mounds of dust softening corners, and they stay there just long enough for you to know you have failed.

I have mostly received the looks, not the compliments. I have felt my face burn, turned away so my guest wouldn't see. I resent this shame, on my own behalf and on behalf of every woman who can't or doesn't want to live up to the Pinterest ideal.

Whenever we were expecting guests, I would spend a frenzied hour or so trying to tidy and clean the most egregious messes. I reasoned that at least I was cleaning somewhat regularly, since we host often. If that's what it took, so be it.

In between, the house would get messier and dirtier. And I would hate it. I like my house to be clean, tidy, and beautiful, for reasons that have nothing to do with shame and social expectations. Achieving my ideal home is complicated by living with a large family, but the more fundamental problem was that I couldn't make myself clean. As with writing, cleaning was something I wanted to do, in an abstract way, but there was always a reason not to.

I tried to believe I was simply busy with more important things, but I knew that wasn't true. I was spending much of my time on activities I did not value. And I was unconvinced, deep down, that taking care of my home was unimportant or that the only reason to do it was to fulfill gendered expectations.

When I was formally diagnosed with autism, it felt like getting my first pair of glasses. The world resolved itself into a kind of sense I didn't even know was possible. Only, this time, it wasn't the external world that became suddenly comprehensible, but my inner world: my reactions, the pain in my body, my emotional patterns, my persistent and intractable challenges.

I spent months reading everything I could find written by autistic people, especially women. I reviewed my entire life with this new light, shining it into the corners and cracks I had never been able to see into or mend. I grieved the ways things might have been easier had I known earlier. Then I set about reorganizing my life.

Much of the process has been a matter of ceasing to throw myself against walls I can't get through and instead trying to find a way around them. Executive dysfunction can make it difficult for me to begin or change tasks, and insignificant decisions, like what to eat for lunch, can completely debilitate me. I've learned to plan a few steps ahead, so I don't have to make decisions in the moment. Life has improved.

Learning about executive function also illuminated my difficulties with starting and continuing to write. Understanding my cognitive processes did help, a little, in working around them.

Setting specific times and attainable goals made it more likely I would actually sit down and write, but I still found myself perpetually distracted, unable to keep my focus even on writing I was excited about.

I also started to learn about sensory processing issues. I could never understand why plates clanking against each other made me want to scream, but I often couldn't hear what my partner was saying next to me. Was my hearing overly acute? Or was it subpar? I was so sensitive to certain tastes but completely incapable of recognizing a flavour out of context. I had no idea why more than half an hour in a mall made me feel lethargic and confused.

It turns out my senses are not the problem, but the way my brain takes in information from them. I enthusiastically set about assisting my own brain. I bought earplugs and noise-cancelling headphones to modulate sound. I started wearing my sunglasses religiously. I accepted that I am not an adventurous eater and began to experiment with the foods I do like. I learned how to use deep pressure, from a helpful friend or a sufficiently solid object, to settle my nervous system. My anxiety dropped precipitously.

Recognizing my sensory sensitivities in some ways made trying to manage homemaking worse; I knew exactly why mess and clutter distressed me and why I had a hard time cleaning, but not how to fix the problem. There was no shortage of house cleaning lists and schedules and chipper articles about how this or that trick vastly cut down on the amount of time she (it's always a she) spent cleaning. Some of the advice was very good. But none of it addressed the actual problem: I felt overwhelmed by the project of maintaining a home. I couldn't convince myself to even start working on it most days.

Then I came upon Laura Calder's *The Inviting Life* while browsing the local library. There is some good practical advice in the book, but what enchanted me was her central premise: her home-making was all organized around her love of hosting. There were no lists or schedules; instead, she talked about how she arranged her furniture and storage so it was easy to entertain. About how she chose what and when to clean to ensure she could comfortably host at any moment, whether she had planned the gathering or not. About how she decorated so that cooking and hosting were pleasant in her space.

I am not nearly as enthusiastic about hosting as Laura Calder is, but the idea of organizing the work of my home around a value or theme appealed to me. It made sense. It created a coherent system out of the many, varied tasks necessary to keep a home clean, tidy, functional, and pleasant. It offered a glimmer of motivation for cleaning and homemaking that wasn't based in shame and gendered expectations.

Watching an episode *of Star Trek: Discovery*, I was struck by a scene in Sarue's quarters, which he had filled with plants from his home world and shaped to his own, alien needs. The Star Trek spaceships are such highly engineered environments that the inhabitants can control the air temperature, light levels, and ambient sounds with a few words. Each crew member personalizes their own quarters, not just with decorations, but by adjusting the environmental controls. *How nice, I thought, to be able to adjust the environment to pleasant levels.*

That idle thought about spaceships at last brought together all the thinking and reading I had been doing about autism and homemaking and writing. I didn't need to live in a spaceship to engineer my environment to better suit my needs.

It may not be quite as charming a concept as Laura Calder's "inviting life," but homemaking to calibrate my environment to stimulate my brain in pleasant and non-overwhelming ways was an exciting thought. What might I achieve in an environment designed for me? I had been very focused, up to that point, on minimizing unpleasant stimuli. I hadn't really considered the possibility of taking advantage of my brain's peculiarities to create positive experiences and improve my capacities.

I started to experiment with my room. I already listened to music almost constantly, so sound engineering was easy. I bought candles and made a linen spray so that the air in my room could be gently and pleasantly scented. I bought an armchair that I can fold myself into, pressing into the arms and the back to get the deep pressure I need to calm myself.

Figuring out how to create regulating visual stimuli proved a lot harder. I could name plenty of specific things I like to look at, but how to arrange a whole room to be visually pleasing and still basically functional? How to minimize the visual distractions that kept me from writing?

I knew I found orderly spaces calming, but that I didn't really like minimalist looks. I was drawn to Victorian styles full of dark colours, intricate patterns, and dramatic shapes. How do you marry such opposite looks? The answer I lit upon was to contain the colours and patterns within tidy lines: I have books and notebooks in bold colours, organized in neat rows. I have my beloved odds and ends in pretty jars. I have unruly plants in the severely rectangular window frame above my bed.

My room, which had always been a haven, became more like an aid; it isn't just an escape, but a space that actively regulates my nervous system and brain. A few minutes alone in my room can make the rest of the day manageable.

Perhaps it should come as no surprise that it is much easier to create when I am well-regulated. I can now sit in my room and write because the room itself both soothes and stimulates my mind without distracting me. When I am not constantly shifting focus because of tasks left undone or disquieting stimuli, I can settle into writing for longer periods of time.

My room only works its magic, though, if it is clean and tidy. The effects, especially the visual effects, don't work if they're muddled by clothes on the bed or dust on my desk.

I had always assumed my main problem with cleaning was motivation-related. But when I experimented with new cleaning supplies, I discovered part of my aversion to cleaning was the sensory experience. I am easily disgusted, which makes certain kinds of cleaning particularly hard, but it had never occurred to me that the cleaning products and supplies were themselves putting me off. A glass bottle is a better sensory experience (for me) than a plastic one. Wood handles on brushes have a solid, rough texture that feels much better than a squishy, slimy sponge. My own cleaning products smell exactly the way I want them to. Cleaning soon became a much more appealing task. Sometimes, now, I clean to help myself regulate through movement and pleasant sensory experiences.

Knowing the benefits of a clean, tidy environment, it's become a lot easier to motivate myself to keep it that way. It has started to feel like self-care. I may not feel like making my bed or tidying or vacuuming, but I know what a gift it will be the next time I walk into my room wanting to write. Supporting my creative pursuits is a much better motivator than shame.

Much of the common wisdom about writing is that you must devote yourself to it, heart and soul. There are many representations of writers as absent-minded, messy, chaotic, even inconsiderate. They are too wrapped up in their art to concern themselves with mundane things like dishes or appointments or politeness. It makes it easy to believe that to be a writer, you must neglect everything else. It makes art seem hopelessly out of reach if there is anything else you value, or simply cannot neglect

I have certainly fallen into the trap of believing I cannot dedicate myself to writing without giving up on other values. That worrying about a clean house, remunerative work, or spending time with friends and family were inevitably distractions from the important work of writing.

I am no longer convinced. I have a full, rich life, and that richness contributes to my writing. It's true, I don't have hours to dedicate to writing every day; some days I don't write at all. But when I do write, I sit down in a home where I feel comfortable and happy. My mind is orderly and calm because I have created a regulating space for myself and put work into keeping it that way. I bring new ideas and experiences to my writing because I also read and sew and have dinner with my family and go for walks with my friends.

My desire to succeed in homemaking is not at odds with my desire to write. Attending to the mundane, including my own well-being, has created more energy for the creative.

M.E. BURNS is an autistic writer, editor, and lawyer who grew up in the interior mountains of British Columbia. In her writing, she explores the boundaries of genre fiction and works out what the good life looks like for autistic people. She lives with her family on the Sunshine Coast of BC, where she enjoys studying languages, dancing, and arguing about grammar and punctuation.

III

Gross Domestic Productivity

The symbolism of birth is used liberally in literature and other art media, but nowhere is it more evident than in the description of the artistic process itself: a writer *conceives* of an idea and *births* a novel, or a painter *creates* a piece, or one might *nurture* the seed of an idea and bring it to *fruition*—words that evoke fecundity, all ripe, as it were, with reproductive imagery. We collectively understand the power of creation, of birth, of rebirth, of the cycle of life—it hits, as the kids today say. And yet, the real-life experience of birthing an actual human baby transmutes the more esoteric concept of creation, i.e., that nearly inexpressible, grandiose, and somewhat overused metaphor, into something quite prosaic. Quite, quite, *quite* prosaic. For there is literally nothing less poetic than a colicky baby at 3:00 AM who has just exploded through his diaper.

Writing this essay and reflecting on what it means to be a mother and a person with creative impulses twenty-six and a bit years after giving birth to my first son, elicited an emotion in me that was quite unexpected and is nearly impossible for me to confess: rage. I am constitutionally afraid of anger, especially my own, and so walking around for many, many days in a funk of fury has left me feeling both exhausted and keyed up. I've been analyzing this anger, trying to understand not only its source, but its target, struggling to nail it down. My inclination is to blame myself (boring), the patriarchy (doubly boring, even if true), cultural and social expectations (see patriarchy), or maybe there's something else altogether.

During this process, I sent a text to a friend confessing this surprising anger, this sadness, wondering if I would have chosen differently if people in my life had been honest with me about what being a mother would all cost (emotionally, mentally, physically). Maybe this lack of informed choice is what's gotten my goat. And it struck me: we were lied to. All parents everywhere were lied to, either directly or through omission. Certainly, the joy and congratulations and excitement that surround the announcement of impending birth seem genuine, even from people who are already parents (the only honest response I ever got was from my father-in-law who just said, "Oh no"). And we find ourselves also complicit in this propaganda—asking about names and birth plans—but frankly (and I don't think I'm alone) when I hear someone is going to have a baby, I feel mostly fatigue. I do, however, keep the secret; I play along, as so many have.

Many years ago, I wrote a feature about war veterans taking their stories with them to the grave—unable or unwilling to talk about the horrors of the battlefields and living conditions of the two world wars. One of the explanations for this, according to a war historian I interviewed for the story, was that often they felt if people heard these stories, they would be shocked into thinking that the sacrifice wasn't worth it, that *their* sacrifice wasn't worth it. Maybe that's why parents don't talk about what it's really like to raise children—especially in Western societies, often alone, often unsupported, and battered by a constant barrage of judgment. We don't want anyone to tell us that our sacrifice wasn't worth it. We raise psychological cenotaphs to our parenting efforts—our children the greatest victory, a hill worth dying on.

Don't get me wrong, I love my kids and there were often moments of joy and deep satisfaction. I didn't hate being a mother.

Possibly this is because I capitulated; I bought into the narrative that any ambitions (artistic, educational) I harboured should be placed into a box with some moth balls and stored away until such time that I was no longer required to be one hundred percent available to two small boys and their multitudinous, never-ending, all-consuming needs. A friend of mine, ten years my junior, says the same thing—all ambitions, all creative endeavours, tucked away ... to bring them out, air them, ponder them, creates longing and maybe resentment, making the work of caring for her two boys (one with special needs) that much harder.

How do I write about parenthood and the impact it has on one's creative expression in a way that is new? Was my situation different? No. Did part of me honestly embrace this excuse to not put myself out there? Maybe. Could I just as easily write about incapacitating perfectionism,* self-doubt, laziness, mental illness? Yes, for they are all a part of me and are something to which many, many artists can relate. As I read through the essays in this anthology that reflect on parenthood and how it both limits our time for creativity while occasionally offering fuel for those impulses, I recognize that my generation—well into second-wave-feminist assumptions, i.e., we *chose* this, eyes wide open, dammit!—was still shackled to a societal expectation that we perform our motherly duties, and that, yes, you can work if you want to—of *course!*—but it'll come at a price. The price was judgment, guilt, anxiety. Damned if you do. Damned if you don't. Maybe this is another source of my anger.

I remember standing in the school yard one day in a circle of moms—there were a few dads who picked up the kids, but the majority were moms. I listened as two or three of the mothers

---

* Oh, that there was another word for *perfectionism*; something that fully captures the obliteration of all creativity or forward movement that this state induces and that also doesn't sound like a humble brag.

discussed another mom who wasn't there—her kids being picked up by the nanny. "I don't understand why [not-there-mom] still works. It's not like she *has* to. It's not like they need the money." Others clucked in agreement—I felt puzzled. I'd like to tell you that I made a joke about the student loans, the years of education that she might not want to have wasted, or the fact that she might like working. But I wonder if I did; maybe I agreed with them. I knew this woman, knew her to be an involved, loving, committed parent who just so happened to have a life outside of her family. Her vocation and parenting were apparently at odds with each other, according to those who were the arbiters of what makes a good parent—correction: *a good mother*. These arbiters may have included me. I had, after all, internalized patriarchal paradigms with little or no analysis for over thirty years at this point.

During this period when I was raising small children, I had the good fortune of being surrounded by many intelligent, artistic women who were in the same boat. One was and is a magnificent potter. An exceptional artist—her unexpected glazes and motifs set her far apart from your run-of-the-mill ceramicist—she stopped throwing pots near the end of her first pregnancy, and nearly two decades would pass before she sat at her wheel again. So many things barred her from her craft—the normal demands of two children, the house that needed running, the food that needed cooking, the dog that needed walking. But what stood out in my memory was her resistance to even attempt to make pots; her fear being that she would be consumed by her art and neglect her children. And then what? And then she would be a bad mother? When I recently asked her about this, she had no memory of thinking or saying this—she said instead that she thought maybe she was just lazy, disorganized, unmotivated. She was none of these things.

When I wrote during the "children" years, it was for money. All of it—no writing occurred for which I wasn't guaranteed payment. A few times a week I would send the children to daycare or preschool, and I would write "advertorials" for the local paper—advertising magazines about Women in Business, Golfing, Automobiles, or Brides. I wrote full-page ad copy for local restaurants and paint stores, and then I got to write features about things that I enjoyed writing about. But understand, without a guaranteed fee, there was no writing. How I found myself justifying putting my children into daycare or nursery school to the stay-at-home moms who made it all look so cozy. I must work! I must earn money—who am I to even breathe on this planet without seeking remuneration for my efforts, leaving my long-suffering spouse to provide.

I said earlier that I capitulated, but I wonder if that's a lie—I am, after all, like many parents, an unreliable witness to my own life (see psychological cenotaph above). I never fully embraced my role as mother; if I'm being honest, most of it was a chore. The title homemaker or (gack!) *housewife* rankled my soul. But if I was going to do this parenting thing, I was going to be the best dang mother anyone had ever seen, dammit! My children were going to be the happiest, most loved, most cherished, most stimulated, most supported, most cared for children who ever walked the earth, even if it killed me. For these two boys became my new project—a fresh page in the typewriter on which I could write the story of the time I did something good. Little did I know then, and what is abundantly clear to me now, is this: Children are not blobs of clay that you get to form into anything you want, or a blank canvas, or fresh sheet of paper. Instead, they're mostly—and sometimes inexpertly—filled-in paint-by-numbers, in colour palettes that don't always go with your decor.

Is there a form of trauma that comes from subverting one's essence for decades? Once those neural pathways are formed and create habits of thought, can they be rewired? Reading other, smarter writers on what used to happen to creative women when shackled by domesticity, it's clear that madness has almost always been one escape. Madness and then valium. And now it's alcohol. (*It's wine o'clock! Mommy Juice!*) What happened to those brilliant women thwarted from pursuing their passions—did they become the bitter old ladies who butt in line at the grocery store (who can blame them?); or like Donna in the TV series, *The Bear* ("It's just hard. I make things beautiful for them. And no one makes things beautiful for me"[1])? I think often of the ladies who were part of a "salon" in the 1950s, whose sole surviving member I interviewed for a feature on book clubs. They did not just sit around and drink wine, as modern book clubs seem to do, but would write whole papers on the chosen books, researching and presenting these papers to the other women. What else was there to do as a professor's wife in 1955?

How many women then? How many oppressed, repressed, depressed women have felt this way; their impotent rage, their formidable creative capabilities squandered in the day-to-day drudgery, spooning nourishment and comfort and order into the domestic maw.

Virginia Woolf, in her essay, "Professions for Women," read to the Women's Service League in 1931, talked about killing the Angel in the House. This "angel"—reference to a self-sacrificing ideal woman in the poem of the same name by Coventry Patmore—according to Woolf, was "intensely sympathetic. She was immensely charming. She was utterly unselfish. She excelled in the difficult arts of family life. She sacrificed herself daily. If there was chicken, she took the leg; if there was a draught she sat in it—in short she was so constituted that she never had a mind or a wish of her own, but preferred to sympathize always with the minds and wishes of others." This angel, Woolf writes, exhorted her to be gentle when reviewing a book written by a man: "be sympathetic, be tender." Woolf proceeds to strangle the angel, her confidence, she says, coming from the knowledge that she was an independent woman of means and felt no need to charm anyone any longer.

"Had I not killed her she would have killed me. She would have plucked the heart out of my writing."

The funniest (saddest?) part of this essay for me is when she says (*in 1931!*): "You who come of a younger and happier generation may not have heard of her—you may not know what I mean by the Angel in the House."[2] Girl, I was born thirty-five years after this address and became a mother sixty-five years after, and I understand who you're talking about. This "angel" existed in my mind, too. But I was not a woman of means; unlike Woolf, I did not have an inheritance from a dearly departed aunt. And I was intensely anxious that if I fussed, if I demanded, if I didn't do all for everyone, the tenuous house of cards that I had built would tumble down, and so I heeded her, the angel in my house.

Remember, too, that it was (the childless) Woolf who said that the only way a woman could write was to have her own money and a room of her own. I sincerely doubt it would have changed anything for me, as buffeted as I was by the winds of judgment (both external and internal); my anxiety and crippling perfectionism would have never permitted me to take that time for myself—as I sat at that imaginary typewriter writing the story of motherhood, there was no chapter where Mommy is anything other than dutiful. In Stacey May Fowles's essay in this anthology entitled, interestingly, "In Defence of Giving Up," she writes of getting out of the house for the first time: "I was excited to be sans very new baby, excited to slip back into the life that was mine before her arrival upended it." Her choice of words, "before her arrival upended it," stand out for me, here. For we mothers are upended, uprooted, rent apart by birth (sometimes literally), and find ourselves on the other side, reassembled into people we don't even recognize. It might be misandrist of me to suggest this, but I don't think fathers experience this, even the most involved of fathers—I don't think they lose themselves the same way. Like a toddler, I stamp my feet and cry, "It's not fair!"

Near the end of my pregnancy with my second son, a group of women gathered at my house. It was becoming a little ritual in the community we lived in at the time—make a belly cast, wish lovely things for the mother and new baby. Schlocky, yes, but also warming as we lit a flame of female friendship around the pregnant woman to stave off the chill spectre of impending childbirth. On this occasion, we were making a mobile to hang above the baby's crib with little talismans from each woman. One friend made me a tiny book, saying that although we were both guilty of turning to books for advice, we needed to learn to trust ourselves. Another childless friend gave me a tiny martini glass as something to "look forward to," when all this pregnancy stuff stopped. But the one thing that stood out, above all others, was a bracelet that a friend had brought back from South Africa, where she'd been visiting her family. She said there was a tribe of women there who, after doing all day—gathering food, working in the fields, preparing meals, tending the children and the home—would gather and make beautiful, beaded things.

I remember having two concurrent thoughts. One: *How wonderful that they have this creative outlet.* And two: *What? Holy shit! I now have to live up to women in a little village in Africa, too? Is it not enough to constantly compare myself to every other woman around me and come up wanting?* If comparison is the thief of joy, my unhappiness is then simply explained. For compare I did—constantly, obsessively. The mom across the street with four kids who always seemed blissful, riding her bike with the trailer attached containing her two girls, while her boys rode their bikes alongside; the very Christian family who didn't own a television and whose youngest son could read complex chapter books in Grade 1; the mother at the breast-feeding drop-in who said that nothing made her baby fall asleep faster than when she read Proust aloud to him (same, doll). Judgments about cloth vs. paper diapers, breast vs. bottle, Ferber vs. family bed, vaccines, organic baby food, organic cotton, attachment parenting, and on and on and on. Everyone else was doing it right. Everyone else was happy. They were in on a secret from which I was left out, like the loner in the school yard, kicking up dust as I shuffled around the baseball diamond with my hood pulled up.

Anna Lee-Popham's upcoming essay in our anthology is the kind of story that makes me want to do it all over again; to really listen to my children and their wisdom, as she does. It is also the kind of story that I would have read as a young mom and thought, *Here's someone who has the secret, too.* I once wrote a feature about things to do with kids in the city we lived in at the time, Kingston. We went to Fort Henry and took a ferry ride to Wolfe Island, we mini-putted at the near-derelict Lake Ontario Park and swam at the community centre, a photographer capturing images of us smiling, the picture of the perfect family unit. A woman wrote a letter to the editor about my story that said, in effect, that my children were so lucky to have us as parents. I thought, *Oh, if only she knew* . . . knew that sometimes I lose my patience, sometimes I raise my voice, sometimes I wish that I could run far, far away and never, ever come back. I wonder now if other moms read my article and felt as I would have had I read Anna's essay during that period of my life. I apologize, then, for perpetuating the myth that it's easier for everyone else.

I wonder, too, maybe if I'd stopped constantly looking outside for validation, if I'd been able to relax and not think that at any moment, when I let my guard down and didn't fear the slippery slope, I would break my children, set them up for failure, ruin them, spoil them; if I could have just comprehended that there's no such thing as a perfect parent because there's no such thing as a perfect person, maybe I could have created space for me to emerge. Maybe the beach ball of resentment that I'd held down with so much effort under the waves of constant doing wouldn't have popped up repeatedly to hit me hard in the face. And maybe—a quarter century plus later—I wouldn't be wrestling with this anger.

Can I reframe these recollections and ease both my rage and my desire to go back and try again (with the accompanying youth and energy that goes with)? My children were the catalysts for much personal growth, after all. They came into my life, trailing their exquisite clouds of glory that made them *them*, despite my efforts to turn them into math geniuses, musical prodigies, or gifted athletes. They held up a mirror to my foibles and forced me to confront my demons. If it weren't for my desire to be the best possible mother I could be, I wouldn't have embarked on the often-painful path toward understanding my various limitations. My mental health was sometimes precarious, and they kept me from the precipice (both metaphorical and literal), they gave me a reason to continue, to survive, and eventually thrive. If they were the living embodiment of my creative impulses during those years, they would read like amateur slam poetry: beautiful, cacophonous, and only fully appreciated by their creator. My umbrage, then, is not directed at the children who make us mothers, but about the systems of oppression, both external and internal that we—or maybe just I—marinated in and failed to question.

As I work through this weeks' long tantrum, it occurs to me that although I wasn't engaged in writing the great Canadian novel during my kids' early years (or any years, honestly—my children were *not* what stopped that from happening), there was a sort of creative process at work. As this anthology reveals, creativity comes in many forms, and it's only our puny human brains' need to define it that ends up limiting it, and ultimately us. Like gathering shiny beach glass, piece by piece over many years, those day-to-day experiences—playing in the park, reading books before bed, road trips blasting music—are likewise collected, becoming a mosaic of the joys and sorrows of the perfectly imperfect life. The gift of hindsight allows me to lift the shroud of anxiety and fear that obscured those days, my children's innate beauty free to shine across the years, my hopes for them, my wishes, my efforts revealing themselves, and in this way and with the profound acceptance that I can't go back in time, I release this anger and vow to be kinder to the person and mother I was.

PAMELA OAKLEY is a writer, editor, and educator who has written for publications such as *Canadian Running, Canadian Cycling,* and *Today's Parent,* among others, and has several features in the *Kingston Whig-Standard.* She currently teaches classes at Seneca Polytechnic, with a focus on food, love, and bad women in literature.

How Can You Write Poetry
If You Don't Go Outside?

Earlier today, I came downstairs to our living room while on a break from an online writing workshop. You were on a break from your kindergarten reading class. Giddy at the possibility of going outside, you said: "You have a break too! Come outside with Dada and me!" I said that I couldn't. That my break was only ten minutes. That I needed to return to the computer soon.

"How can you write poetry, Mama," you said, "if you don't go outside?"

We're a year into this pandemic. Next week it is officially spring and we've both been in virtual school since September—you in kindergarten and me in an MFA in Creative Writing. While initially you mostly stayed attentive, delighted by the chance to engage with peers and a teacher and structured learning, you have recently grown fidgety, explaining that it's just too much screen time. When you say this, I cringe, then remember Adrienne Rich: "The institution of motherhood finds all mothers more or less guilty of having failed their children."[1]

Like you, I have been growing more restless. I've been careening between the side tasks of a writing life—submitting grants, applying to barely paying internships, editing other writers' work, listening to audiobooks while I cook dinner or squeeze in a short run. But when it comes to writing, the act that makes one a writer, I'm hardly doing it. The days fill up quickly with time spent refocusing your attention on your math class and then dishes and emails, and I find myself drained at night. I feel disconnected from my curiosity.

Tonight, I look out on Toronto, this lonely city in lockdown. This city of all-night ambulance sirens and skinny coyotes in the cemetery up the street. Beyond my window to the west, Toronto's CN Tower alights: green and red lights shimmy into the night sky and flick to blue and purple as they descend. This urban display of extravagance makes the once-tallest structure in the world look impressive, the lights ending at the bulbous centre that holds a gravity-defying glass floor. But the tower also looks garish, a phallic misfortune in a city that, last week, demolished wooden structures built for people living in parks a year into a global pandemic. This dichotomy also exists in my relationship to this city: I'm drawn to it, this city of bright lights and so very many people. This city where I was born and where I returned so I could raise you close to family. I'm also often repelled by this city, its everyday violence always on display and its constant reminders of my mother's death.

Tonight, I think back to your words: *How can you write poetry, Mama, if you don't go outside?* I realize we both need breaks longer than ten minutes between lessons. I decide you will not log on to virtual school next week. Instead, each day we will go on adventures in this city. We will move more slowly and watch the world around us. I will write about whatever comes forward.

Monday

On the first day of our week of adventures, your little voice pulls me from the deep fog of morning slumber. You call out from your bed, saying you are cold, and I stumble from sleep into your room and tug your sheet up over your small body. You would have done that yourself, you explain, but the sheet was tangled around your legs. I kiss your forehead. You always look so still in these early mornings. Still so small in your growing body.

"I love you," I say and tuck you in.

"I love you too," you say.

"Sweet dreams."

"Sweet dreams to you too."

I love this echo you create in these early mornings. Your voice calm and quiet, manipulating the language only slightly to turn it into a reply.

"Time to sleep," I say.

"Time to sleep you too."

But I am rarely able to get back to sleep at this early morning hour. I take tepid steps down our creaky stairs and sit on the couch beside your small desk, easing into a still-quiet home in the still-quiet of a pre-dawn city. I open a computer to this essay -in-progress and look at the pieces I've written: about mothering and writing, education and capitalism. I try to conjure up the questions— the backbone—that will guide it to something whole. But it all seems blurry and incoherent. I have been looking to past writers: Audre Lorde, James Baldwin, Adrienne Rich, Paulo Freire. But whenever I bring in their vibrant words, I feel something is lost in translation. Like I am trying to force the expansiveness of their writing into a rigid shape. I hope our week of adventures will help me create something comprehensible, or at least help me reconnect with my curiosity.

An hour later, when you come down for breakfast, you are a swirl of constant questions about language and animals and words.

"Who named the vegetables first?" you ask. Then, before I can think of a possible answer—"Also, who named the animals first? The animals might have had different names before. Like fox. What was the name for fox before fox?"

I think of the Brazilian educator and philosopher Paulo Freire, who said: "My question is how to make clear to the students that there is no such thing named biology in itself."[2]

I say: "I don't know . . . But different languages have different names for fox."

You tilt your head to one side, pensive but momentarily satisfied. Then—

"What's the French word for fox?"

I think of my twelve years in public school, staring out the windows of French Immersion classrooms.

"Well . . . I can think of the French word for snail."

"What's that?"

"Escargot."

Your eyes open to this sound. You repeat each syllable aloud slowly, turning them into English words: *yes-car-go.*" Sounds and words with such fast connotations in English, but meaning such a slow-moving, oozing being in French. You seem intrigued. Then—

"How are superbats made?"

It is then I notice that the shirt and pants of your pyjamas are both on backward. The tags sticking up subtly. I tousle your hair.

Later, we drive to Crothers Woods to collect rocks. The moment we arrive you take off, a suddenly unleashed five-year-old. You run, up and down paths and through mud, giggling as you navigate trails non-stop for forty minutes. Then we pause to sip water and listen to a woodpecker. You look in amazement at the bird, a surprisingly small one, tapping its beak again and again on the tree trunk. *Rat-tat-tat-tat.* You are fascinated. Then you point to a squirrel—

"Look, a squirrel!"

Then to a piece of cement in the path—

"Look, sidewalk! How did it get here?!"

I delight at your eagerness and wonder if I might find some of my own in these crooks and corners of life outdoors. I think of the speed at which your curiosity wanes when you are faced with the computer. You, such an avid learner, turn stagnant in front of a screen. Freire said that students become glassy-eyed and checked-out when they are seen as receptacles into which knowledge is placed. I wonder what invites in my curiosity, and how I might write so as to not expect my readers to be receptacles.

Tuesday

This morning when you come down for breakfast, I am sitting in front of the computer again. You ask what I'm doing.

"Writing. Slowly. The writing is going very slowly."

"As long as you're living, you're learning. As long as you're learning, you're reading. As long as you're reading, you're writing."

You say this quickly, your tongue pulling on the rhythm between the words. The first part of this proverb is one you devised a few months ago, a few months into virtual school, when you were feeling frustrated that you hadn't said a correct answer in class. I appreciate that you have added two more sentences to it for my sake. I try to remember if I've been talking with you about the relationship between reading and writing, or perhaps your teacher has. Though you have come up with such maxims on your own before, words that I would immediately doubt came from a five-year-old mouth if I hadn't written them down the moment they emerged.

When you sit down to eat, you ask what I'm writing. I tell you I need to send a nonfiction essay to my classmates by Sunday, and I'm having difficulty pulling together the pieces I've written into a story.

"Well. Help them help you."

"Okay," I say. I realize I'm open to any suggestions.

You take a bite of scrambled egg, then say, "You need to ask them: Can you help me do this? You need to ask them if they have had that problem before."

"Oh, yeah?" I feel a bit uncertain. "And then I should ask them what they have done?"

"Yes." You stop eating and hold your fork upright in the air, pensively. "And then they can help you with that." When you say this, you point your fork toward the wall. I imagine my non-existent story written there in invisible ink I can't read.

You say, "Does that sound like a good thing for you?" Then you point your fork at me.

"Yes." I pause. "Have you ever had that problem?" I want this conversation to continue.

"What problem?"

"You know, the problem of not being able to think of a story."

"Oh. I don't think I've ever had that problem."

"Have you had other problems with stories?" I hope this is good parenting and not just the desperation of a dry writer.

You pause. "Sometimes I forget the story."

"Yeah. And then what do you do?"

"Then I just try to remember." You are back to taking bites of your breakfast and say this nonchalantly.

"And is there anything that helps you?"

"Not really anything. Sometimes I just wait . . ."

Something in me relaxes minutely.

". . . until, um, I can remember."

"That seems like good advice."

I sit back in my chair. Then—

"Which one is nonfiction again?"

Last week, I sat with you while your teacher talked about stories. At the end of the lesson, your teacher asked the class which kind of stories were nonfiction. "True stories!" twenty four- and five-year-olds shouted through their screens. When the teacher asked which were fiction, the class chorused: "Imaginary stories!" But you are always mixing them up. I relish this, remembering how Aleksandar Hemon said that, in Bosnian, there are no words for fiction and nonfiction. "Literary text," he wrote, "is not defined by its relation to truth or imagination."[3]

Wednesday

This morning, I am writing. The words are coming. Some emerge feeling bloated with meaning, too heavy with history to fit into the structure of a sentence. English, though it's my mother language and the only language I write in, seems always limited. I think of Adrienne Rich: "This is the oppressor's language / Yet I need it to talk to you."[4] I keep writing.

After you come downstairs, we drive to see your grandad and nan, my father and stepmother, in the west end of the city. We walk to a playground near their place, and you let out a squeal when you see it. You are immediately in motion. My dad and I sit and talk about the vaccine and the dining room at their retirement home opening again. You run and run and run. Circling back to see us, every ten minutes or so, sweaty and delighted, oblivious to your face mask. Another child comes to the playground and you approach each other, both stopping six feet away.

You ask: "Do you wanna play?"

Then you chase each other around and around. When you both land on the swings to catch your breath, you ask her name and she says her name and then signs it. Then she asks, "What's your name?" You have been learning the basics of sign language and you move the fingers on your right hand in the shape of each of the letters.

I wonder if you feel that language is limited or if it expands out for you, always providing more ways you can communicate what you mean, more ways for you to tell stories.

Thursday

Today we go to visit a tree in the east end of Toronto where there is a plaque for my mum, your nana. We decide we will plant bulbs. Dahlias, whose vibrant colours your nana loved. I glance at you in the rear-view mirror while we drive past the hospital where my mother died, and I think of your uncle and I singing to her there—our creative renditions of songs from *Rent* and *Les Mis* and other musicals we grew up with. When we arrive at the beach, I park and as soon as I open the door and unbuckle you, you are out. Shivering and delighted by the wind off Lake Ontario.

"A beach!" you shout.

I'm surprised by your amazement. Surely I mentioned where we were going? Your look says there is a difference between me saying the word beach and the feeling of the wind from the lake on your face.

"Sand!"

We navigate across bike paths to get to the boardwalk. When we find the tree, it is much taller than when we were last here. You, too, are much taller than when we were last here. The tree looks sturdy, its trunk seems to be thickening proudly. Its arms reaching out and up, skyward, not unlike my tall mother once did. I pick up your child-sized shovel and start to dig small holes, careful not to dislodge the bulbs we planted in previous years. They are starting to peak through the soil. You pick up a hand trowel and follow me. You toss the bulbs in the holes we dig, then we adjust them so their roots are pointing down.

You tell me: "In my superbats' world, bulb roots can grow both up and down. All the way through the earth. All the way up to the sky."

Dirt embeds itself quickly into the knees of my jeans. I feel content. A few women stop and chat. I try seeing us through their eyes: a forty-year-old woman with her five-year-old child, planting bulbs to commemorate a grandmother. All this seems like a beautiful, excruciatingly normal course of events, untinged by the specific grief of my mother dying when I was eighteen. A grief that has muzzled me for much of my life.

When we finish planting bulbs, we run in the sand and you climb on the rocks.

"Look, I'm in a circus!" you call out. "Listen to me sing!"

Then you shout out to the waves, your voice cascading through high and low notes. I hear myself exhaling. Toronto's wind seems to whisper: *Twenty-two years was a long time to hold your breath.*

Friday

This morning, I'm writing. Over breakfast, we decide to go for a walk in a local cemetery. As we get ready, your voice calls down from your bedroom:

"What clothes should I wear? Is it more like winter today or more like summer?"

"I put some clothes out on your bed that will work well for today." I'm distracted, trying to wrap up emails on my laptop in the kitchen while pulling together snacks before we head out.

"But did you check what it feels like outside?"

"Yep, I went out on the back porch." I'd left the porch door open, and a cool spring breeze seems to be beckoning as it enters the kitchen.

"But what about the weather out the other door."

I pause, looking up from the computer screen. "It's the same weather."

"But it might be sunnier out the front door!"

I think of the different ways to enter this essay. I consider walking through the doorways it seems to offer and seeing what happens on the other side, allowing the doorways to lead me to where the story is going, opening in different directions toward my own curiosity.

This afternoon, you do a virtual dance class to a song from *Hamilton: An American Musical*. You've been fascinated by the musical for months. The rhythm of the language. The talk of revolution. As you learn to fan your hands as exclamation points to "The Schuyler Sisters" song on the Zoom dance class, I listen to a talk by Dhruv Jani, the founder of a game and arts studio and an interactive story designer. He talks about the possibilities of interactive fiction as a repudiation of the white saviour narrative, a space of plurality against the legacy of colonialism, and hypertext as a way to communicate dissent. He speaks to how any time we engage with story we change it.[5] I wonder if everything becomes fiction in the retelling. When I read what I have written in this essay there is an order, a logic, a clarity that has only come through revision. All the words are true, the actions, the events, the emotions, but I have chosen what to include and what to avoid so that in the writing and reading of this, I can understand myself, my child, my mother, my parenting in ways that help me understand my life. This telling, all telling, is partial. As author and memoirist Ayelet Tsabari says, memoir is a curation.

Saturday

When I go into your bedroom this morning to pull up the sheet, you greet me with: "I love you, Mama."

I have come up to your room from my perch in front of my laptop, where I was writing this essay, to you, perhaps also to my mum. "I love you," I say.

"Mama, what's my name upside down?" I smile. I tell you it's still time to sleep.

I go downstairs and return to writing. The words come quickly and I can hear the undertone, the cadence, of the sentences. I rush to capture them. More come.

Shortly after breakfast, you, your dad, and I drive to Rouge Hill. On our way, we listen to the *Hamilton* and *Cats* soundtracks. You sing along. When we arrive, you are a bustle of lyrics. Mixing the two musicals—"Aaron Burr" becomes "Aaron Purr"—and coming up with your own lyrics. You, like your uncle and like me, aren't bound to the words that have been previously sung.

As we walk along the paths with other people and dogs trying to get some time away from the specific claustrophobia of the pandemic in the city, you spot an opening between trees off to the side of the path and pull us toward it. We walk down the small path, and we're suddenly in a quiet forest. We walk deeper into the forest, away from people and dogs. Almost, it feels, away from the pandemic. We spend much of the day here, exploring steep hills and a stream that runs between some of the trees.

As we are walking back toward the main path, your dad and I walking ahead, you call out from behind.

"Look! What is all this?"

We come back to you and look around. Beneath your feet and spreading out is a large patch of small curlicue growths emerging from the ground. They seem to be unrolling like spirals. We all crouch down. We pull up Google and research. It's a large patch of fiddleheads, the edible heads of young ferns that can only be harvested for a week or two before they unfurl.

We take some home for dinner and you delight in each bite. After dinner, we call your grandparents and you exclaim: "Guess what we found?!"

Before they can answer, you say: "I'll give you a hint: It's something you harvest and you have to get it when it's ready and it's only ready at a specific time. A time like now."

I think there is something important in this I can learn about patience and writing.

Sunday

This morning, I am writing. I am up early and writing. This morning, and throughout the day, I turn this essay into something coherent; I turn words into poetry. I take a break and we go outside, your dad, you, and me. You grab a hold of both of our hands as we walk through the park, swinging your legs out in front of you and back behind you.

"Look," you say. "I can fly! I'm a superbat!"

Over dinner, I tell you that you get to go back to virtual school tomorrow. You'll get to see your school friends and your teacher. "Are you excited?" I ask.

"Yeah!" Then your face falls slightly—"Wait," you say. "That's only exciting for me if we get to continue to do these things."

"What things?" I ask.

"Like harvesting fiddleheads and going on adventures outside." I agree.

ANNA LEE-POPHAM is a poet, writer, and editor in Tkaronto (Toronto). She holds an MFA in Creative Writing from the University of Guelph, and is a graduate of The Writer's Studio at Simon Fraser University and University of Toronto's School of Continuing Education Creative Writing Certificate program, where she received the Janice Colbert Poetry Award. Her writing has been first runner-up in PRISM international's Pacific Poetry Prize, shortlisted for The Fiddlehead Creative Nonfiction Contest and Room's Poetry Contest, and longlisted for the CBC nonfiction prize, and has been recently published in Arc, Brick, Riddle Fence, Canthius, Autostraddle, and others. Her debut poetry collection, Empires of the Everyday, was published by McClelland & Stewart in Spring 2024.

Creating Outside the Boxes

Sometimes we as humans go to great lengths to attach ourselves to things we believe identify who we are and that validate our existence. Sometimes we don't even realize that's what we are doing. Like willingly filling out forms that require us to check off certain boxes about ourselves. Without a second thought, we eagerly grab the pen (or the mouse) and start ticking away, box after box. Black . . . check. Canadian . . . check. Consciously or unconsciously, those boxes make us feel like we belong somewhere. It's when we step outside of those boxes, or don't fit into them, or simply reject the idea of them, that we become the rebels. The radicals. The misfits. The disruptors. I am a disruptor. I wasn't always this way. I, too, have twisted myself into pretzels trying to fit inside those boxes.

I'm sure many recall those long-held notions about left- and right-brained people. Those who were creative were thought to be right-brained. And those who were analytical were seen as left-brained. It was made clear that we were only solely one or the other. After all, the research said so. But that belief has been largely debunked. We had been self-identifying, ticking yet another box. Right-brained . . . check. Being led to believe I never belonged in both, it now makes sense that this notion was not based in science, but was rather a cultural observation. I had no evidence that there could be an in between, but now I know that in between exists. That we can be, and we are, both.

An opening statement from the Healthline website, based on the research of psychobiologist Roger Sperry, reads: "The theory is that people are either left-brained or right-brained, meaning that one side of their brain is dominant. If you're mostly analytical and methodical in your thinking, you're said to be left-brained. If you tend to be more creative or artistic, you're thought to be right-brained."[1]

There is no in between in this statement. And if you reject this theory, pull it apart, or challenge it, you are a disruptor. Creatives like me are disruptors. We fit where we fit. I married young, had children young, completed a few degrees young. I was living inside the busyness of a path that many of my friends had not even embarked upon yet. I was a twenty-four-year-old married mother of three small kids. By twenty-eight, I had four. None of my friends wanted that. I was logical, but there was also a serious, creative art to making that life work.

The hectic, daily chaos that involved being creative in order to make things function, also involved the real necessity to plan down to the minute, analyze every situation for the next time, and be methodical in the day-to-day responsibilities of parenthood. Life was one big mathematical formula. If I drop one kid off at soccer practice by four, factor in the fifteen-minute drive to buy lunch supplies, subtract the Tuesday carpool time, and allow for traffic time coming back to the field, my child won't be the last one standing with his coach waiting for pickup.

My mind wasn't contemplating Sperry's position back then. I wasn't musing about how different parts of our brain help us accomplish different tasks. I was aware of how some experts separated the logistical and the analytical (handling bank accounts and solving problems) from the creative and the imaginative (viewed as frivolous time spent on empty leisurely pursuits). But

I and many others were certainly the exception to the rule. My brain, my body, my soul—they were all one, working in unison. No separation. The same skills that I used to plan my chaotic life were the same ones I used to plan my next creative piece of work.

The realization of this likely came once my children were grown and the ink had dried on my divorce papers. I had the benefit of reflection and hindsight. As an artist, content creator, and habitual contract worker, I now realize my entire arts career (which was always happening in the shadows of the work I did to pay the bills) was steeped in strategic planning, calculated risk, and methodical decision making that would hopefully lead to a declaration of artist as my realized profession.

As a Black person working in deeply colonialized spaces. As a Canadian existing on stolen and unceded Indigenous land. As a female drowning under a patriarchal system that determines the worth of my productivity. As a young mother who raised four children amidst often frenzied schedules. As an adult worker in the gig economy without the security of pensions and benefits. In reverence to all of these parts that I am, I will no longer accept that the work I do as a creative is not intrinsically tied to the parts of me that practise in analytical and methodical thinking. Or that I must separate the left side of my brain from the right when my work as a creative is so complex and so intricately wrapped around my logical and strategically planned productivity. I'm not talking about the economically stable, mostly Eurocentric, male dominated definition of productivity. But rather what I and all creative minds know (or should know) to be the true definition of what it means to be productive.

For writers, two hours of deep thought plus one page of writing is productive. For visual artists, three months of planning plus three days of creating is productive. For a performer, one hundred hours of practice plus thirty minutes of performance is productive.

Behind all of that creativity lies the anchor (or logistics) of finding time and space, of planning and charting the path, of being methodical and consistent in the creative delivery.

When my children were small, it was logical and necessary to plan the time to write and create, and to find the spaces in which to do it. Whether that was finding library time, or slotting in creative moments during the kids' school hours. When can the babysitter show up to relieve me on a Saturday afternoon so I can attend that writer's workshop? Did I factor in enough travel time to do a drop off and get to a quiet space to create? These things are not associated with the act of being creative yet are the necessary means to that end. I had to analyze my situation and then go into planning mode in order to exercise my art. That is vital.

And when one looks at it that way, the left and right sides of my brain are not separate from each other. They are in cahoots with each other. I don't believe we exist inside one box or the other, when these things are so intrinsically linked. I am not a right-brained person or a left-brained person in those scenarios. I create outside of those boxes.

When my four children were in elementary school, I was in the throes of a social work degree. I was also a freelance writer, which sometimes meant putting in a lot of hours of research and writing to create the story. Often it felt like working for free. My then-husband worked in construction, which meant early hours and late nights. So, the freedom to be creative often came down to questions about how to plan ahead and work out all the moving parts we called life.

Back then, I took a job working in a youth homeless shelter doing overnight shifts, because it worked best for my life at that time. I would put the children to bed by 8:00 PM, then head to work for a ten-hour awake shift. I would return home by 7:00 AM the next morning to relieve my husband for his job, get the children off to school, then try to get a few hours of sleep. There was a small window of time in the day where I could write and create—sometimes between laundry loads or before school was over. After supper it was homework, baths, and the bedtime routine. Then I was back to my overnight shift again. Wash, rinse, and repeat.

I lived inside those moments, but I never stopped to reflect on them as they were happening. However, if I were to look at it now from my former husband's perspective, I think it must have been quite challenging for him, snoring with a house full of sleeping children while I was awake and working at the shelter; getting up as early as he did to eat breakfast and fill his lunch box; travelling to work, grinding all day, then coming home to supper already waiting for him. It must have been brutal. I say it this way not to be facetious or insinuate that he didn't help out. But rather to point out that I was living in the old-fashioned notion of roles. The idea of turning off, concentrating on your work, or being productive must have looked much different for him than it did for me.

In our male-dominated, colonialist, patriarchal society, where males have statistically held the benefit of stable daytime work and perhaps a partner who took care of the bulk of the children's needs, the freedom to be creative might be very dissimilar for a single parent, or a household consisting of two gig workers trying to balance the bills. There's no attempt here on my part to make one sweeping, blanketed observation about one type of worker, as our lives are all very complicated and deeply involved. But this type of worker—you know, the one with a full-time secured job, benefits, and a retirement plan—has historically been accepted as the norm we must all strive for. It is the most traditional. The most credible.

Embarking on an acting career, the writing life, or other creative pursuits, whether full time or not, is unfortunately sometimes still seen as less respectable, or squandering your potential. Our norm continues to dictate the conventions that define productivity. And, in doing so, has systemically ignored the realities of the work that goes into being creative. We do not fit into that traditional box. Yet our endeavours, no matter how we logically approach them, are in fact an extraordinary example of the so-called left-brained ability to be productive. Most of the work that went into my ability to be creative involved attention to detail, juggling little people and tight schedules, and finding ways to allocate the time and space for artistic endeavours.

Robert H. Shmerling, MD, Senior Faculty Editor with Harvard Health Publishing, said that notions of left- and right-brainedness are widespread and widely accepted. But that they are likely wrong. In his 2019 article, "Right brain/left brain, right?" he says that it's true that some functions exist on various sides of the brain, which we know based on evidence, and that specific areas of the brain are affected after an injury; for example, the parts of the brain that become impaired after a stroke, or how damage sustained to the back of the brain can cause blindness. But when it comes to deeply embedded notions of who we are based on which side of our brain is dominant, the disruptor in me says we are not the box we appear to fit into. Our creative minds are just as vital, important, and valid as the logical mind. Shmerling agrees, we are not one or the other. We belong in both of these boxes:

> But for more individual personality traits, such as creativity or a tendency toward the rational rather than the intuitive, there has been little or no evidence supporting a residence in one area of the brain. In fact, if you performed a CT scan, MRI scan, or even an autopsy on the brain of a mathematician and compared it to the brain of an artist, it's unlikely you'd find much difference. And if you did the same for one thousand mathematicians and artists, it's unlikely that any clear pattern of difference in brain structure would emerge.[2]

The notion that we are either only logical or only creative has been challenged, debunked, and discarded. This should be a relief to those of us who experience barriers to prescriptive narratives around productivity vs. creativity. No longer should we as creatives be expected to abandon all else (children, unstable work priorities, and so on) for the sake of creativity in order to be seen as productive. We must acknowledge that these come together as a package, and that we cannot separate our challenges and barriers from our ability to be productive. We need to embrace this as our reality and understand that our ways of being creative, expressing our artistry, and getting the work done, look different for each of us.

Even writing retreats have caught on. Some have included spaces for parents with children and are finding other creative ways to remove historic barriers to artistic endeavours. All this time I had been making it work. Before motherhood, during motherhood, and once the nest was empty. What a realization. We can and we do make creativity work.

The issue then becomes, how do we as artists take this a step further, so that our creative work is less about whether we have been productive (although we know the work involved was productive) and more about the process of expressing our creative freedoms? About being immersed in the work that brings us joy and inspiration simply for the sake of feeling joyful and inspired, without the baggage of guilt and pressure that's often associated with having a finished project to show for it at the other end?

I think part of the solution lies in breaking free from the idea that your productivity is only demonstrated by the outcome of your artistic efforts. Artistic work is not obligated to end in a result. It should be noncommittal. It should be okay to create for the sake of creating. Putting the baby to bed, finding the time to attend a week-long retreat, or working habitual contract jobs (even if there is no long-term financial security) must all be seen as a natural part of our creative productivity, because it is. And it should go beyond doing it because we think we are expected to. It should mean doing it as a recognition of the fact that both sides of our brains are simultaneously at work.

I am often asked how I find the time to write books, do research, create magazine features, teach college, mentor emerging writers, and develop new screenplays. There was a time when the ability to do those things was almost non-existent for me. When I felt tremendous pressure to shut off the world and just create; I felt forced to find tiny pockets of time where I could. When I worked those overnight shifts at the group home, I would grab some time in between doing room checks.

I was always chasing time, desperate for opportunities to slip my memory stick into a computer and bang out a few sentences. That's because I was always pursuing the end goal, otherwise I felt I was not being productive. The effort always had to end in a final piece of work, polished and completed. Something had to come out of it or else it felt wrong. I now approach the work with a belief that the process of just creating is my productivity. The end result—if I get there—is the bonus.

I have learned over the years that my work as a creative is not bound by the unattainable and superficial lines drawn around the purpose of my work. I have come to terms with the fact that my art is sometimes existing because I just want to feel joy in that moment. Exhausting, because I am on the grind by choice. Rewarding, because I am in the throes of what makes me happy. Inspired, because my work has the potential to bring someone else enjoyment. Even if that piece of work never sees the light of day, I have already seen its light. Sometimes that's only for me, and in that case, it's enough. Sometimes that's for the world, and in that case, it's everything.

I am resolved that no matter who or what my art is for, I am an unconventional, non-conforming artist creating without apology. Rejecting notions that suggest I can easily shut off the outside world and be productive in my purpose for creating is incredibly cathartic. The fact that I have started a piece of work to begin with automatically indicates a process of productivity. Stepping outside of the superficial boxes and staying there is freeing. And rejecting the notion that the right and left sides of my brain do not collaborate with each other when it comes to creativity and my creative process is incredibly liberating.

WANDA TAYLOR is an award-winning author, screenwriter, journalist, and college professor. She writes fiction and nonfiction across children's and adult markets. Her book *The Grover School Pledge* received the 2023 Northern Lights Middle Grade Book of the Year Award. Wanda's essays and poems appear in anthologies across North America and the UK. Her bylines appear in numerous publications, including the *Globe and Mail*, *Quill & Quire*, *Atlantic Books Today*, and *Black2Business Magazine*. Wanda is a Faculty/Mentor for Kings Writing and Publishing program, and teaches courses in journalism, creative nonfiction, screenwriting, and documentary film at Centennial College. Wanda is a recipient of the Women of Excellence Award for Arts and Culture.

ADELLE PURDHAM

Turning Down Syndrome into Art

*The reward of art is not fame or success but intoxication. And that
is why so many bad artists are unable to live without it.*
—Cyril Connolly, critic

*I'm often caught between dueling convictions:
I want to mother and be something other.*
—Liz Scheid, *The Shape of Blue: Notes on Loss,
Language, Motherhood & Fear*

As writers and artists, we become explorers of our hearts. "You
work from what you have," Sheila Heti wrote in her fictionalized
account of life as an artist.[1] What I have, what I have always had, is
an abundance of emotion. Where does that emotion go, swirling
inside me, when I am not feeling it? At five years old, my youngest
daughter asked my husband: "When do rivers end?"

"At a lake or ocean," he responded.

"But what about the ones that don't go to more water," she wondered. "Where do they go? Underground, maybe?"

Hard feelings can fester if you let them. Emotions that go un-
expressed stay underground, trapped beneath our skin. When we
release our feelings, do they seep out through our pores, evaporate
into the air, and reform above us like clouds? Clouds of emotion.

And when it rains, one simply needs to find a comfortable spot, a patch of grass or a mossy cushion, on which to lay down and soak them back in.

"Are those piddows from the rain?" the same daughter, then three years old, once asked me. *Puddles* came out as *piddows*. And in my head, rain piddows became rain pillows, a wet and quiet place to rest your head. Everything is material for the artist. Soak it up, and then write it down.

Perhaps emotions that come and go are like ideas floating in the air. Ideas hovering around, looking for a place to land, a receiver. When I'm busy caring for children, these apparitions haunt my mind; they hover in waiting like lost souls looking to become embodied through thought and language. Without the bandwidth to think—with children occupying that space—their howls echo like wind through an empty corridor. And my mind aches, as though grieving a loss for something that never was.

Lessons from the margins of motherhood:

One, you don't get to choose your children; they arrive.

Two, they may or may not be like you.

Three, you will love each of them differently, for their unique gifts, but also the same. To love each according to their needs is to understand that those needs will not be equal; that concepts of "fair" and "equal" are different.

When my daughter with Down syndrome was born, she needed surgery. The scene, post-surgery, is a difficult one to relay. I saw a helpless vessel lying inside the hospital's isolette, out of reach, her broken body fragile as glass. A fresh, raised scar bisected her abdomen, tubes coming out of her tiny nose, from her arms and legs, and electrical leads protruding from her chest. She dropped to four pounds then, four days old, an ethereal weight to the world, kept both sedated and alive by medication, held here by every ounce of my heart. Later, when I was allowed to hold her, I stroked her downy cheek, tucked my long finger across the width of her palm, and recognized her instantly as my own. I was the good enough mother, as D.W. Winnicott first described, and she was well held, meaning, she would forget me as she grew older.[2] As a woman who was well held as a baby, I've learned self-love. By extension, that love metamorphosed into every one of my children.

During my pregnancy, I experienced grief, rage—*Why me? Why our family?*—sadness, confusion, love, and happiness. The day after we received her diagnosis, my husband and I boarded a plane to Barbados for a friend's wedding.

"We don't have to tell anyone yet," my husband said.

I didn't want it to be a secret. In Barbados, I sent my emotions out to sea. I sat on the beach and I wrote in the new blue journal I'd picked up at the airport, my tears staining the pages. I chose blue for how I was feeling. Writing in pregnancy allowed me to process feelings of grief and heartache, and to peer deep into the well of myself and ask, *Who am I now?* With the healing sun, words against the page, and the unconditional love of my husband, the hurtful feelings dissipated; they passed by like ill-formed ideas. My heartbreak was filled, every crack and crevasse, with love for my unborn daughter.

Once I accepted her diagnosis, and she was born, it haunted me that another parent might not know, after receiving a similar prenatal diagnosis, how much I loved her; how much a child with Down syndrome is deserving of love. That society still didn't know—or care—how much I loved my daughter. The simple act of loving a disabled child was, as Heather Lanier explained, "counter-cultural."[3] Without giving a parent the time and space to understand that love—really feel it—the losses would continue to pile up.

I once perceived Down syndrome as ugly and undesirable, but even when I carried a fetus with Down syndrome in my womb, I never perceived myself that way. Now I know differently. Former versions of myself are ugly and undesirable to me now. With my daughter's arrival, I came to understand something about what it means to be ableist. I continue learning. I saw my daughter's beauty. I heard it in her laugh, the sound of a tinkling bell. And I knew, as a writer, something else. What we perceive as ugly or undesirable is rarely made into art. And all I've wanted, from the moment she first existed, what every parent wants, was for my daughter to have a full life. To be fully included and experience joy. First, I had to make Down syndrome into something beautiful in my mind to be able to explain it to others, which meant truly seeing my daughter for her inherent value. To turn Down syndrome into art was a way for me to process the impact of her life during those initial days when I was uncertain. What greater gift of understanding could there be?

Motherhood inhibits creativity by overtaking the mind with thoughts of children whose spirits are strong and whose howls are loud and persistent. In the eleven years that I've been both a writer and a mother, I've learned the best way to work is to banish myself. To disappear. Find a door to close and ghost them. Ideas need digesting, and no matter how hungry I am, no thoughts will appear on the page when my plate is full, with no time to eat.

My children bring out my emotions most forcefully. Do they pull them from thin air or straight from my heart? That combination of love and rage. Love. *Are those piddows from the rain?* Her hand clasping mine. Rage. *Why do my children have to act like animals in public?* We once travelled to Japan as a family and ate dripping ice cream cones on the side of a sacred path. One didn't like her ice cream flavour and proceeded to cry. Another, holding a different flavour, devoured her cone as fast as she could so she wouldn't have to share. The third offered to share her cone with the first, who'd eaten no ice cream. But as she stretched out to pass the cone to its new owner, the child who scarfed hers down snatched the half-eaten cone and gulped it down in one bite like a hungry wolf. The shopkeeper's daughter who sold us our ice creams, a young Japanese girl approximately the same age as the wolf, heard the fuss and offered the end bits of broken cones to the crying child. The wolf snatched them from her hands and gobbled them up, as the one with no ice cream howled louder and my eyes blazed red. A group of Latina grandmothers sitting beside us tsked at me in disgust. The sacrilege. *At least,* I thought, *this would be something to write about.*

The dual reality: Children hinder the creative process, but they can also be an inspiration. They are often the ones who bring me to my subject. We took our first steps together; me, into writing, them, into the world. Our outward mobility intertwined. Three chevrons shape the black tattoo on my wrist, symbolizing a tripling of the twenty-first chromosome that characterizes Down syndrome. The tops of the three arrows point toward the sky for upward momentum, a reminder to keep the social movement going in the right direction. I permanently inked my skin, creating art out of love for my daughter; should it surprise then that she would inspire the creation of a memoir, ink on the page?

"Oh god," another woman writer once said to me, when I explained how having my daughter changed my life. "Don't tell me your book is about how you wouldn't be where you are if it wasn't for her because I don't buy it."

Mothers are often denied their feelings and truths. Why? Because, as essayist Alicia Elliott points out, mothers are one of the most hated groups in the world.[4] If the way I felt toward a group of people shifted after my daughter arrived, isn't that worth writing about? But that wasn't exactly what my friend was getting at when pressed. It wasn't that she didn't perceive Down syndrome or motherhood as art-worthy; it was that she believed I would have come to my current world view without ever having conceived a child with Down syndrome. She preferred to consider me a writer, to deny motherhood's role. She wanted me to be the sole proprietor of my own life. But my children staked their claim in pregnancy, cut into the soft root of my flesh, took with them what belonged to both of us when they unearthed themselves from my being. What they removed when they departed were thin slivers of my heart. Heart slivers that developed, like the transplanted limb of a geranium, flowering into a new bulb. A whole new velvety being.

As a woman with children who is also a writer, it's as though I'm divided in two. The mother and the writer; two separate identities that don't intersect. But that division is also a source of contention. A mother who writes? A writer who mothers? As Eula Biss points out, women's "personal, bounded individuality is compromised by their bodies' troubling talent for making other bodies . . . One of our functions, as women, is to be divided."[5] Every day of my life, I feel divided—between giving my children what they want and giving myself what I need. Those goals are not at odds; they cross over. I want my children to get what they need; they need their mother to get what she wants.

In that divide, between the selves of mother and writer, I envision a glass pool where my emotions reside. When the water is still on calm days, I can see to the bottom and access my rational thoughts. When the wind kicks up on emotionally charged days, the swells muddy the depths, making my true self unclear. When writing proved difficult, Hemingway consoled himself by thinking "All you have to do is write one true sentence."[6] To write it true, I need to be able to see clearly. How to explain to writers without children what I have learned from raising my babies? Like any life experience, the influence of my children makes my work whole.

While my children commandeer a large swath of my emotional energy, I might as well put what is left, the by-product of that, to good use.

I've learned to take that swell of emotion, the blaze behind my eyes, and turn it into art.

To be divided is to possess two hearts, one beating inside my chest and the other outside of me manifested as my children. The love was there when my firstborn arrived, but as an explorer of my own heart, I excavated more closely and could better see how we are interconnected when my daughter with Down syndrome was born. Her life illuminated sediment in ways and colours previously unimaginable simply through the magnitude of my feelings for her. I should never have been surprised by the ferocity of my love, and what could be more beautiful than that? More art-worthy? A mother's love; our foundation.

But how do you take Down syndrome, the raw material, and turn it into art? By examining the heart, I've learned. By feeling through what is there with your bare hands. By waiting until the water stills and peering deep in the pool to the bottom of your true self. By asking, *Why is it that I fear the other?* I was not the one considered disabled, but when it felt like a part of me was, I could see the world from two sides: how I looked at disability before and how I wanted the world to see my daughter, the way I see her now. She is a child, as luminescent with possibility as any other. The writer in me knows Down syndrome is rarely written about in literature, and not in a favourable light. The mother in me knows I write in the dark to make my daughter's light seen.

Would I love her the same? I wanted to know when I carried her inside me, the heft of her body weighing down my melon-shaped abdomen. Love can be hard to peg, effusive. Describe it? I'm not sure if I can. But maybe I can show you, by writing about the pictures of my mind, what it feels like to be awestruck, inhabited by something larger, to contain boundaries of the self that spill over.

Perhaps I can describe the music I heard floating in the air like creative energy as I carried her life inside me: *Life will never be the same.* That note sang to me repeatedly, whispered in my ear on the beach and echoed through my mind for the duration of writing my memoir, changing its timbre, moving from bass to baritone, the heavy notes of the cello sustained, reaching to soprano, the sweetest sound. That song echoed so I wouldn't let it go until I'd written it cleanly on the page. Until it became a theme in my book. Until I realized something Audre Lorde wrote, that it is only through our differences and acknowledging those differences that change can happen.[7] And what we need—what I needed—was to change how we perceive people with Down syndrome. I needed to change and grow to become a writer and mother worthy of my daughter. I would love her the same as I loved my other daughters, but the feelings and experiences for each of my children's births were distinct, and that made them worth writing about. I only needed to defend the existence of one of my children.

Down syndrome became art-worthy in my eyes. How had I missed this before?

Lessons I have learned as a writer:

Write it true, listen to your heart, listen to your heart, listen to your heart.

As writers engage in writing, what we undergo is a metamorphosis. Faced with plain rock, the collection of our experiences needs chiselling, whittling down through the intense process of knocking out words, hammering into the stone, one tap at a time. I reach that love through my experiences, the well of emotion, or by tapping into creativity, literally pulling ideas that appear from thin air, by trusting in the universe's offerings.

One day, I woke up thinking that I wanted a necklace to wear with a new dress I had purchased the day before. Where did the thought arrive from, and why did it appear? I have no idea. But the thought that I would buy a necklace existed that day. My husband and I were on vacation in a quaint touristy town, and we planned to walk through the historic quarter. We happened upon a jeweller, and I tried on two different necklaces, but neither sang to me in a song I recognized. We pressed on and arrived at The Upper Canada Native Art Gallery, where I opted to look at the Indigenous artwork on display inside. While scanning a stand of necklaces, I had the feeling of eyes burrowing into the back of my neck and felt compelled to turn around. When I did, I saw the metallic glint from across the room. Later, the shopkeeper would insist that the sparkling light chose me.

I crossed the room to study the light and saw the unique carving of what looked to be a wolf engraved on a tear-drop pendant.

"Is it a wolf?" I asked the shopkeeper, who pulled the necklace out from behind the glass showcase for me to inspect closer.

"I believe it's the raven," she said, "but let me double-check."

But before she flipped the tag over, I knew the lyrics to this long-forgotten song. I'd heard it before. It was a raven, all right. Ravens are known tricksters; hand it to a raven to appear wolf-like.

I held the necklace up to my neck, admiring its copper shine in the mirror, and the shopkeeper appeared by my side.

"I hope you don't mind," she said. "I just had to see that colour against your skin. I knew it would be perfect. May I?" She clasped the sterling silver chain, letting it hang against my collarbones, and made a joke about being grateful for the oversized clasp with her aging eyes.

"I've never seen the necklace shine like that for anyone," she said. "As you came in, it was drawn to your energy. That necklace chose you. I know this may sound funny," she acknowledged, "if you're not used to talking about energies."

I blushed, bowed my head, and stared curiously at the talisman around my neck. And somehow, regardless of how salesy she may have sounded, her words rang true.

I bought the necklace.

On our walk back to the car afterward, I asked my husband, a scientifically minded skeptic and occasional cynic, what he thought of the exchange.

"She was being genuine," he said. We left it at that.

When they come from a place of light, our truths become indisputable.

My raven necklace laid under the glass in the shop beside a hummingbird pendant, the delicate birds that were always my grandmother's favourite. My grandmother hung a feeder outside her kitchen window, and she would call me there as a child to show me her visitors and their fast-beating wings. After her death, the appearance of hummingbirds, real or other, kept my mom and I linked to her. Hummingbirds became an evanescent touchpoint; they embodied my grandmother's song. I picked up the hummingbird necklace and bought it for my mom.

Whose energy was in the room at the Native shop? Mine, my grandmothers, both? Where did each of my children come from? Did they choose me? I hope so. I would choose them if I could.

Does it matter where we draw our inspiration? As writers, does it matter where the energy comes from, as long as it arrives? For me, that source is my love for my children. And that love was passed down to me through generations of women. Clouds are made of water and water can hold memories. And so it was, the clouds that hovered above me that day held showers of my grandmother's love.

Our emotions endure through time. While I sent my grief out to sea in Barbados, that's not to say it has never found its way back to me. Grief, that deep sorrow woven with strands of sadness, unfurls itself eventually, and like any emotion, those strands know how to find their way home. Occasionally, I forget what I've learned and lapse into old ways of thinking, such as faulty notions of good or bad—simplified dichotomies—instead of accepting our complexity with an openness free of judgment. Writing is a way to brighten, clarify, and help me remember, or further examine, who I am or want to be. In writing, I diversify.

My emotions are a flowing river that cycles back. When the emotions return, I let them. After the rain comes, I lay down on the earth and soak them back in and then write the scenarios that stirred them up in the first place, that muddied the pool. My emotions are one of the most useful tools that I have when I consider what to write about.

In the car, I pulled out my phone and looked up meanings of the raven in local Indigenous storytelling. Two significant interpretations popped up. I was pleased to find the first was the raven as trickster. *That's why I thought you were a wolf,* I chastised the engraved copper medallion, smooth against my hand. Similarly, I had once believed that those with Down syndrome were something they are not. But the other meaning I hadn't known. That before there was anything, ravens were the creators of light. Ravens are creators of light.

As a mother, I am the raven, birthing my children, creating light, and because I am divided and they carry my heart, children are also creators of light. They are replicas but also wholly new.

As a writer, I am also the raven, forming art from darkness, pulling from a place where before there was nothingness—turning life into light. Life is a song, and "the song is for singing," wrote poet Wendell Berry.[8]

My daughter is the one who taught me to see differently and who inspired me to create from light. We were once one, yet now we are divided. The light that only she could shine on the world has become love. I'm thinking about how her love passes through me and then divides itself into my stories, multiplies and grows stronger still. That love brightens and transmutes into stories on the page. And that is how art is created through love and light, which is, of course, life. And that is how you turn Down syndrome—something beautiful, my daughter—into art.

ADELLE PURDHAM is the author of the memoir-in-essays *I Don't Do Disability and Other Lies I've Told Myself* (Dundurn Press, 2024). She holds an MFA in Creative Nonfiction Writing from The University of King's College and is a qualified French teacher. She is also a graduate of the Humber College Creative Writing by Correspondence program. Her prose and poetry appear in literary journals, anthologies, magazines, newspapers, and online. As founder of The Write Retreat, Adelle facilitates workshops for women writers to create. She lives and writes in her hometown, Peterborough/Nogojiwanong, Ontario, and teaches creative writing as a sessional Course Instructor at Trent University. Visit her online: adellepurdham.ca.

Hummingbird

I learned early the power of silence. At three years old, I could send my father into conniptions by not saying good morning. I'd peek out at him from behind my mother's legs as my older brother begged in his mind for me to "just say good morning" so he could eat his breakfast in peace. (I'd observed how the world worked "from small.") To excuse such unwieldy behaviours, this girl-child was given the label "shy."

Over time, I noted where else silence sat, and there, it was not powerful. It was a rumble of roiling discontent, dismay, confusion, and bewilderment. Sometimes, it was rage. I noted a pact of silence, of not telling, amongst women: Do not tell pregnant women that mothering is hard or that you will be blamed for all things inconvenient or difficult for men, children, and other wild things. We tell other women instead that they glow. We do not tell girls that mothering and art is next to impossible. Instead, we watch them draw and dance and swirl—and give them music lessons and watercolours and a plethora of brushes.

My mother painted for the first time in 1973. She tells me she did it with a Q-tip using a tin of watercolours from her children's stash of art supplies. Both of my brothers and I had been furnished with pastels, paints, inks, and drawing pads, as it was known that art was good for the children. The twelve hard circles of dried compacted pigments had names like Sky Blue, Deep Green, Crimson Red, and Burnt Sienna. She softened the colours with drops of water from a small glass at her side.

Did the Q-tip provide the texture she wanted, or did she not have time, agency to leave and find the right paintbrush, one perhaps a step above our plastic bristles? Was this improvisation a search for the right texture on paper, a quest for something previously untouched by our play, or was it yet another "make do"—a denial of self? Why this sudden urge to express something ephemeral, to create something concrete from it and place it into the world?

She is ninety now, remembers clearly and answers.

Her painting was of a man on a bike who passed by the gate as she sat on the front porch at our home in Blue Basin, Trinidad. A minute, brightly coloured hummingbird hovered just above his head. She had not painted before.

"It was just an impulse," she said.

Where is the painting?

"I don't know, I was never in one spot long enough to continue anything. It is hard to track anything when you move all the time."

In my mother's case, the married state meant the impulse to create was held down, held back, undernourished. She carried the world and was too busy when the flash of a quest for artmaking awoke briefly in her being.

"I was the centre of keeping the kids going," she said. It meant that all obvious physical signs of her art disappeared as we left one house and set up in another, over and over again, following my father's career to Trinidad and back to Canada and to the various postings in between and around those oceanic moves. I asked her what she had been looking for by picking up that Q-tip to paint.

"Liberation," she said.

Advice

I found an essay entitled, "How to be an Artist, according to Georgia O'Keefe," written by Alexxa Gotthardt. O'Keefe had a daily routine, with much time alone in her studio. She wrote once to a friend, "I was at work before eight—stopped a couple of hours at noon—then at it again till six—I will be at it again tomorrow."[1] The essay mentions the efficiencies of ritual and neatness and the organization of space. I think the greatest efficiencies lie within the Single Mother Artist who still manages to write one line of a poem sometime within a six-month span. And it is a good line. The hardest part to learn is to be okay with one line when there is space for nothing else. It may be difficult to calm the yearning and not pine too much for more time and energy, to be okay with the beautiful phrase crafted in the mind while sitting/working/feeding/managing. The most efficient use of the creative impulse, sometimes, is to harness it, and tell it to wait, while you keep self and others alive. Metro. Boulot. Dodo. Work. Feed. Fall down. Then act in corners of time. Sometimes, to be efficient, it is best to eat an orange, feel the sweet nectar drip from your lips, and onto your neck, and down beneath your tired clothing and then, for one second, bird-like—look up.

I advise one to carry a notebook at all times—a small one that does not take up much space on your person or in your thoughts because your being is required elsewhere.

I advise one to sit facing the door on the subway. You can see who walks on for the most part, except at St. George Station where the doors open on the other side. This public transit state of vigilance is common amongst most Black people, many women, and mothers travelling with children of any age. This positioning allows oneself a modicum less anxiety in a public place under the constant weight of the gaze of others. It allows one to stay vigilant but with a fleeting freedom, where you disappear into a phrase.

Write out your worries first in the notebook, I'd say. Spill out all the concerns about food, foyer, and family court. After you've done that and perhaps found a temporary respite, the art will come. It always does. You just don't know if you'll get to the end of your worries before disembarkment at Eglinton Station where you do mindless work to pay for the food, foyer, and family court. Maybe by then you will have written a phrase. If so, it is a good art day. Maybe it is even a beautiful phrase.

Accept long fallow periods. This is also artistic work. You must wait. Until someone stops banging on the door, until the child stops crying, until you can breathe again. Eat. Go outside, if you can. Walk the city streets for a second or two—whatever is available to you—if the children are old enough for you to do this. Otherwise, stay put during these fallow periods. Dance. Sing. Wait. Hold. Hold. Hold. Until until until. The being rests and builds up inspiration and courage and when "all full up," as it feels to me, produces a creative act. One poem. A flourish of an arm.

Oh . . . and carry a seed. I mean it. Carry a seed in your left hand, or your right. Paint your belly in magnificent colours under your clothes, to help remember who you are. The time will arise again in a glorious panache, if only for one second or a few.

The discipline is holding against the pull of distraction that would keep you immobilized. Note how you are held under. Note how you were held back. Note that is not your failure. Acknowledge the energy expended while also navigating Blackness through colonialist structures and the mentalities that embolden them. See how some imagine their own injury as they cause harm, as they try to silence you with their shivering tears. See clearly who might try to shut you down. There are those who would let you drown. Write, dance through to the other side of this knowing. Something lies there. It can be beauty. It could be art. The discipline is kindness to self when none of this is possible. The discipline is forgiving yourself when you cannot do it all and lying down to rest, if only for a moment.

Awake even earlier. This is time no one can tread on. Until they do. It is not the existence of men, children, and other wild things that will kill you. It is expectation and entitlement, a social understanding that you are not a Self and that you must give your All away, even your silence. Otherwise, you are stealing.

Ask your significant people to be holders, protectors of your space. Together, create the structure within which you make your art. If they will not/cannot, find your own way.

Have at least one Jacqueline—the friend who says, "I know your life is shit and you have no time. Do not lose yourself. I want from you one piece a month for one year on anything." This friend gives you assignments and then publishes them. "Take yourself seriously," she says. "They won't. Before you leave for the long commute to work, print out these musings. There might be space to edit on the way. Put pen to paper." Sometimes I take a laptop, however, that requires a whole other level of awareness on public transport. Either way, I work in short bursts. I move from metaphor to metaphor. I sip quickly, locate a glorious moment and breathe in. If you can do none of this on some days, listen and watch the others on transit as they move, sleep, think, feel.

Keep everything. Well. Most of it. When you move, place your art in a box. Never let it out of your sight. Sometimes, all you will do is look at it sideways at night, over there on the shelf as you fall into an exhausted slumber. There is a power in holding bits of yourself and carrying your own house on your back.

One year, I pulled everything out of that box. Twenty-year-old poems, an unreleased album of songs, clippings of published poems, performances, classes, various bands of my own making and those of others. I pulled strands of myself that lay scattered around the corners of my life on clusters of yellowing paper. I pulled together all those whispers and brought them forward. Once gathered, they looked like a thing, an identity that I could share as a whole, more than murmurings from a corner of a desk in the dark, more than writing "on the side."

Once we were grown, she did try it again. My mother. Painting. One summer afternoon, this time in suburban Ottawa, I noted that she'd bought some paints, brushes, a couple of small canvases and placed them in a corner of the basement. I understood that to paint, one needed light and a place to set up an easel. The enormous, darkened room filled with cardboard boxes, filled with ideas of belonging that we'd dragged from house to house, was not conducive to such things.

Bird Song

Early mornings, I wander around my Toronto neighbourhood, walking Jazz, my golden, curly haired spaniel-poodle mix, sipping coffee. I then make my way back home, knowing I've taken care of an important aspect of being. This ritual is part of a long series of artistic acts, so subtle that they are unrecognizable as such from the exterior of self. I know, however, that strands are forming out of ether and that soon, I will raise my hand, make a fist, and pull them—a sentence, a word, a paragraph, a lifeline—forward into this place.

It is minute choices that determine if a woman lives or dies, whether or not her soul stays entirely her own. Often, we give these moments away or they are stolen and mount into carnivorous years. We then drag ourselves onward with hearts emptied of blood. We awaken suddenly, fully depleted without art, without breath, with no legacy other than the worldly accomplishments of others.

Even though I have never heard hummingbirds sing, I imagine that they do. I imagine my mother, the painter, racing from colour to colour, sipping the nectars of love and art, moving with wings that flutter so rapidly they are invisible.

GLORIA BLIZZARD, a Black Canadian woman of multiple heritages, is an award-winning writer and poet. Her work has received the Malahat Review Open Season Creative Nonfiction prize, has been nominated for the Queen Mary Wasafiri Life Writing prize and the Pushcart Prize. Essays, poetry, reviews and poetry have been published in the *Humber Literary Review, Musicworks, Wholenote,* the CBC, and ByBlacks. Gloria holds an MFA from the University of King's College. Her book of essays, *Black Cake, Turtle Soup, and Other Dilemmas,* is published by Dundurn Press.

IV

I Artsy

Writers. Painters. Poets.

Indeed, as we have seen, artists across all media universally experience a profound internal pressure to generate our "creative things." When we fail to meet our creative goals, we are overwhelmed by guilt and self-criticism. While these feelings can affect everyone, they are particularly insidious for artists and are amplified in those with mental or physical health challenges. The self-imposed pressure to create art further intensifies the burden for those juggling extensive parental and career obligations.

Making matters worse, an artist's natural tendency toward self-doubt is compounded by a heightened susceptibility to imposter syndrome. And I, a scientist, am not immune. When I started the MFA program with my fellow co-editors, I resisted labelling myself a writer, let alone an artist. After all, compared to my colleagues, I had only academic publications to measure my writing abilities. It was as if my status as a writer was tied to my earnings (or lack thereof) from published creative work. I felt awkward and intimidated by those with substantial bylines and author credits. I tried to learn from them, though. The literature they liked or books they offered me must be good, right? However, I often found these books and articles tough to read, understand, and enjoy. I was put off by the creatively expressive narrative and abstract metaphors.

Artsy was my term for them. I had morphed *artist* into a word of derision, an insult—as if it was bad to have an expressive, creative flair or be too much of an artist.

It didn't dawn on me until much later that my lack of confidence in identifying as an artist was proportional to the time spent immersed in my new craft. It reminded me of how I felt during my early days in a research laboratory, clumsily setting up my first experiments. It's a wonder I didn't get a bill from my supervisor for broken glassware. Unlike writing, if I made mistakes, feedback was immediate. My supervisor didn't hesitate to interrupt and put me on the right track. Artists don't have that option. The creative thing is often not shared until it has been tweaked and teased by its creator into near-perfect form. Usually, long swaths of time pass before we are ready to make ourselves vulnerable to feedback. The learning curve for becoming a scientist may be steep, but at least it's well-delineated. Creating is amorphous and intuitive.

Developing artistic skills often takes a back seat to family commitments or a full-time career. Non-creative pursuits don't have the luxury of procrastination. A parent can't ignore a crying child. The calls from a friend in crisis must be answered. The scientist must focus on experiments or risk losing their research funding. The artist must struggle to achieve perfection or even proficiency in their craft because circumstances prevent consistent practice.

Throughout this collection, we've seen that interruptions come in various forms. I particularly related to the essays where health challenges hindered one's capacity to do the creative thing. While writing my first book, I developed a chronic pain condition that, at times, compromised my ability to write. I worked in front of a computer for more than ten hours daily. Facing a deadline with my publisher, I began my day at 5:00 AM to finish my book's first draft. Then, at 9:00 AM, I went to my research office at the hospital and spent most of the time working on the computer there. Poor posture, stress, and age-related degeneration all coalesced into horrific chronic neck pain. I was miserable and unbearable to be around. I was like the cranky lion with a thorn stuck in its paw. I also began to dread my book. At a time when I should be celebrating its imminent publication, I was mired in pain and anxiety. The only reason my chronic health issue was resolved, ironically, was because of the pandemic. The lockdowns altered everyone's work routine, and the shift to working from home eliminated the ergonomic disaster known as my hospital workstation.

My health failed me a second time after I began working on my next creative thing, a novel. I was excited and enthusiastic, carefully planning my work strategy and setting word count goals. Then life got in the way. I came down with another debilitating health issue, the main symptoms being profound nausea and extreme fatigue. At its peak, I could only work from my bed. If it hadn't been for the lockdowns, I would have certainly been on medical leave. To this day, I still don't know exactly what was wrong because the burden of the pandemic delayed the proper diagnostic tests, but the best medical guess was that I had an ulcer. Creatively, I was devoid of inspiration and completely unproductive for months.

As I started to improve, I became obsessed with finding optimal workflows, creativity hacks and apps that made my creative work more effortless. Since my mind felt foggy and muddled, I sought out techniques to capture and catalogue research for my novel. I even enrolled in Tiago Forte's Building a Second Brain course. If his methods allowed him to collect and remember everything important, maybe it would save me too. I gobbled up books like *Atomic Habits, Deep Work*, and *Getting Things Done.* I felt encouraged and emboldened each time I finished reading a book, as if I had discovered the secret to finally getting my creative things done. The same thing happened with the countless books on writing by prolific authors sharing their secrets to success.

The problem? You can't schedule creativity. Or rather, you can (and should), but the main issue was how I made myself feel after inevitably falling short of my forecasted word count. Repeatedly. Rigid to-do lists and word counts weren't working for me. I had become fixated on the mechanics rather than the craft.

The best advice I gleaned was from a YouTube video profiling the writing routines of famous authors. Paraphrasing Neil Gaiman's routine (among many others): You must show up for yourself and your art. Show up and sit at the ready. You aren't allowed any distractions, except perhaps a window to the outside world. No phones, no open browser windows, nothing. Just you and your art. Even if you end up sitting and staring into space, or in my case, at the blinking cursor, the mere act of devoted time will make room for working on your creative thing. Eventually, Gaiman muses, you will get bored of sitting there and get down to creating. What I found so powerful from this advice was the lack of expectation. If you wind up with nothing, try again tomorrow. Whether you end up with a few words or pages, both are considered successes.

After my failure with productivity apps and methods, I wondered how so many others, mere mortals compared to the godlike Authors I had been studying, could successfully navigate creative minefields and produce meaningful art, especially those confronting more significant barriers to creative expression and profound obstructions based on their circumstances. Even with my career demands and chronic pain issues, I knew I came from a place of exceptional privilege. I had a full-time career paying the bills, a home, and a supportive, creative network. Although I am part of the LGBTQ+ community, my workplace is openly accepting, and as an adult white male, I haven't felt threatened or intimidated since the early 1990s. I have never been made to feel the bias and systemic discrimination experienced by the BIPOC communities or had to circumvent barriers challenging those with permanent physical or neurologically diverse conditions. When Gillian came to our writing group with the idea for this collection, we all immediately knew it was a creative thing that had to be made and put into the world.

It was fascinating to see how the essays touched each of us differently. While some seemingly didn't apply in a current circumstance, others profoundly resonated. The upcoming essay by Keriann McGoogan, a fellow scientist, particularly struck a chord with me. Through her experience, it dawned on me that my struggle to identify as a writer or artist because of an inferior skillset was wrong all along! The skills used by a scientist were the same as those of a writer. Both have developed keen observation skills, carefully document and capture even the most minute detail, and explore and experiment with their work until it succeeds. If I could use the robust skills I had developed and apply them to my creative projects, then perhaps others could see how to leverage what they use daily for their creative work.

It was also clear from this collection that regardless of the individual experience, artistic creation was happening all the time, even when we weren't sitting down, dedicating time and energy to focus on our creative outlet. One of our favourite expressions in writer's group is "everything is copy," meaning that no matter what happens to us in the day, from the ups and downs, the best to the worst, the experiences and people can all be used in our craft. Suddenly, that obnoxious store clerk, rude subway passenger, or frail older woman shuffling around in the park feeding pigeons will share snippets of their personality with future characters in a novel.

Often, writers get the advice to "write what you know," but I prefer to think of it as "use what you know." This means applying your everyday skills and habits to fuel your creative endeavours. Set Shuter's forthcoming essay echoes this sentiment, emphasizing that finding time for creativity doesn't require large blocks of uninterrupted time. I've learned that capturing thirty minutes here and there, whether on the subway or in a quiet lunchtime corner, can be just as effective. These brief periods for sketching, writing, journaling, or simply contemplating can keep the creative fire alive. Rest is just as vital. Meditating or sitting in silence can open doors to unexpected inspiration.

It's also easy to get lost down an internet rabbit hole, seeking the best advice, like my obsession with searching for the optimal productivity workflow. Ultimately, I learned to pick and choose advice that felt right in the moment. Importantly, we must remember why we picked up the pen, paintbrush, or whatever the craft tool may be. For me, it was for the love of the art and the joy of creating something meaningful to me.

I remember a pivotal experience during the MFA program as I put together the first chapter of my nonfiction project. Something remarkable happened. I lost all track of time, and every so often, a tingly wave of excitement swept over me when perfect sentences came to mind, dialogue I wanted to include snapped into place, or a sudden insight improved faltering prose. Afterward, I felt accomplished, like I had solved a complex puzzle.

I would later discover others called this "creative flow" or would say they were "in the zone." I had a simpler explanation. It was joyfulness. These were moments where I got lost in the creative thing, and it didn't feel like work or an assignment. I was writing because I was meant to tell this story. Put simply, I was having fun.

I began to chase this feeling, but the more consumed I became with setting word count milestones and deadlines, the fewer and fewer of those moments of euphoric creation occurred. The pressures of self-expectations sabotage our joy. I now realize that if I want to write and experience these moments, then removing self-expectations is the surest way to be in the moment and foster joy in my craft.

As I read the essays in this collection, I felt the collective joy in creating emerge from their stories. That was my answer to finding inspiration for the creative thing. Feeling joy is now my barometer for creative work and is my antidote to toxic productivity. Each essay contributor faced barriers to their creative expression, whether self-imposed or because of circumstances, and found ways to rediscover joyfulness to elevate and overcome them. Often, all that's needed is a shift in perspective.

Put another way, we turn obstacles into opportunities.

CHRISTIAN SMITH holds a doctorate in the molecular and cellular biology of cancer from the University of Toronto, has over two decades of experience as a research scientist, and since 2006, has held the position of Manager of Research Operations at the world-renowned Brain Tumour Research Centre in Toronto. Compelled by an insatiable drive to learn new things and challenge himself, Christian returned to graduate studies and completed an MFA in Creative Nonfiction from the University of King's College in 2017. With luck and an incredible writing community at his back, Christian published his debut nonfiction book, *The Scientist and the Psychic: A Son's Exploration of His Mother's Gift*, with Penguin Random House Canada in December 2020.

SET L. SHUTER

How I Stay Creative
While Working My Ass Off
(For Someone Else's Art)

I'm standing alone in a dark closet of a film studio, lit only by my computer screen and flashing blue lights from the hard drives connected to my machine. It's my sixth day working, and I've been here for sixteen hours. The coffee beside me, I think it's my fifth of the day, is cold and almost empty. The craft truck has long since closed its doors and driven off. I'm starving as I watch the footage from my latest commercial render the dailies to be delivered to the editor. I'm alone with only forty-five minutes left to go. Soon I'll get in my car and drive home to the comfort of my bed.

My phone dings. There's an email waiting for me from someone I've never met. This stranger wants to hire me for their next feature film starting next week and was sent my way by a former colleague. I say yes because I always do, even though I haven't seen my family in over a month. What filmmaker can afford to resist the opportunity for more work?

"Hi, there. Thanks for getting in touch. Yes, I'm interested and available."

As a freelance filmmaker working in the Canadian entertainment industry, I've had the privilege of being paid to make movies for almost ten years. To grow up and become the version of myself that I dreamt about as a girl is a dream come true—I spent countless hours as a teenager ignoring my homework to watch every horror movie I could get my hands on between endless waves of sitcoms that projected from a fourteen-inch CRT. I foolishly dreamt I'd grow up and become an actress like Jamie Lee Curtis and Anjelica Huston, or maybe a TV writer. Although things didn't work out the way I imagined, I never could have expected to have the career I have now and the one-of-a-kind adventures it has taken me on, because I didn't know it existed.

Since my first and only day on set as a production assistant serving coffee, I've worn many hats on feature films, television shows, and commercials, mainly in production as a digital imaging technician, and post-production as a video engineer and digital colourist. These positions are highly technical and require significant brainpower, overtime, and multi-tasking to be done effectively. They are also disproportionately occupied by men.

While I haven't become a TV writer (There's still time! I'm not dead yet!), I am a writer and have been for most of my life. From writing and performing sketches in elementary school to joining The Second City Training Centre in my early twenties, then finding my place in writing literary essays and pursuing an MFA, there is a creative side to me that exists outside of my line of work in a creative industry.

My writing life is naturally unpredictable because my career requires most of my time and energy. Depending on the project, working on film sets usually lasts twelve or more hours each day for days, weeks, or even months at a time, and often in strange or unexpected places ranging from a box at the Rogers Centre to a flimsy tent blowing in the wind on a busy downtown Toronto street. If the production requires travel, I may also find myself living in a hotel room away from my desk.

I have lived in motels in Sudbury, North Bay, and Sault Ste. Marie for months at a time, slept on the floor of a remote cottage, and driven all night to get to where I need to be for productions. If I'm working in post-production, the hours vary depending on the project and the deadline for a festival or broadcaster—I could have a breezy eight-hour day five days a week for a few weeks or work seven days a week for as many hours as it takes to deliver on time. This can mean I sleep at my desk, or if there is a technical problem, I work longer than I hoped and have to kill plans I'd made for later in the day.

As a result of the consistently inconsistent nature of my career, I've had to squeeze every word of my creative projects between takes in studios or supervised client sessions, ever-changing locations, and on my rare days off. Scheduling time to write is not a luxury I am often afforded due to the unstable nature of my profession.

What does this mean for my creativity?

As a chronically ill woman without a nest egg or wealthy boomer parents to bankroll my endeavours in the inflated hellscape that is the 2020s, to continue to be creative, I must set boundaries between my writing and work, carve out a work-art-life balance when possible, and approach my filmmaking gigs as if I'm purchasing my days off to guarantee myself writing time. If this were a mathematical equation, the variables I consider are whether it's the busy or slow season in the film industry, how much money I have saved, and whether my savings can cover my fixed expenses.

Of course, this all depends on whether I am physically capable of working.

Despite my gruelling hours at work, I considered myself lucky to have few obstacles to my writing. I don't have a husband or children, but I have a low-maintenance partner who works full-time to support himself and a codependent rescue cat who screams at me when he wants something, any time of day.

All of this changed when I got sick.

I was diagnosed with rheumatoid arthritis (RA) when I was twenty-eight years old, six years into my film career. This happened when my fingers fused to my steering wheel after driving home from a freezing fourteen-hour day spent working in the back of a cube truck in a December snowstorm. Once my partner pried each finger free one by one, I was referred to a rheumatologist who held my hands in his and delivered the life-changing news: I have a disease; there is no cure. It will almost certainly worsen and eventually cripple my hands if I don't take my medication. From that moment on, my life would never be the same.

A new nightmarish world was waiting for me, one full of medications for a degenerative chronic inflammatory disease and the unavoidable side effects. I was put on hydroxychloroquine (for which the Cheeto with a bad wig the Americans elected as their forty-fifth president created a drug shortage) and then methotrexate, a nasty drug that does the job, but takes more from a patient than it gives and is used in many chemotherapy cocktails. Then there were the TNF inhibiting injections to which I had an allergic reaction: in a day, I lost all sensation in my hands—this lasted for weeks and could have put me into cardiac arrest if I'd taken my third dose instead of going to the hospital. The fear that I would never feel anything in my hands again, not my cat's fur, the heat when I touched my partner's cheek, the cold Atlantic Ocean on my skin, terrified me.

During this dark period, I wasn't able to lift more than ten pounds and was told I couldn't work without doing irreparable damage to the joints in my hands and the brittle bones of my fingers keeping them in place. Movements I once took for granted, like the clicking of a mouse, sent searing pain through my fingers, up my arms and then landed in the back of my neck. The pain was so deep I'd work myself into a frenzy and want to lash out by punching something. I didn't qualify for disability and even if I had, the amount is pathetic and not livable, but luckily* I'd acquired a line of credit before I quit my full-time post-production job a year earlier. It was easier to live off it than go into credit card debt to pay my rent.

For the next two years, I had to make extreme lifestyle, diet, and work-related changes for my body to heal. Stress is a significant trigger for this illness, as are inflammatory foods, which film crews are often fed on set. If I continued to live the way I was before my diagnosis—long hours, overnight shoots, not taking breaks between jobs, saying yes to every offer, eating fast food all the time, partying as stress relief, borderline burnout every day of my life—I would never achieve remission. As a bonus, I would have to up my doses of the unpleasant drugs that allowed me to function while leaving me with nausea, hair loss, insomnia, migraines, gastrointestinal problems, and liver toxicity. You get the point. Fun stuff. Continuing with my previous lifestyle also meant that I would not be able to write. Take it from me, the most powerful creativity vampire is physical pain. Setting boundaries was necessary if I wanted to return to work and be creative.

The Covid-19 pandemic, as catastrophic as it is, allowed me to make changes without the extreme pressure of going back to work. The hustler's mentality prevalent in the film industry evaporated when almost everyone I knew in the industry was unemployed

---

* By luckily, I don't mean to imply that going into debt as a disabled person is luck. I mean to say that it was pure luck that I experienced a lesser of two financial evils before my income-earning potential took a hit.

for the foreseeable future. I finally caught a financial break for a few months because I qualified for CERB (Canadian Emergency Response Benefit).

Once the lockdown on the film industry ended in Ontario, I wanted to try returning to work. My first job was a commercial for a bank I'm not allowed to name. I was terrified, not only because I worried about damaging my hands but because I hadn't been on a set in so long that I didn't know if I remembered how to socialize with my peers, let alone colour correct footage to the liking of the cinematographer. Reputation is everything in the entertainment industry, and I couldn't bear the thought of destroying the career I'd worked myself into illness to build.

Not one single day is the same when working on set. I had no idea what to expect once I walked onto location and had trouble staying asleep before my alarm clock went off at 5:30 AM. My anxiety turned out to be unwarranted because, like riding a bike, my instincts kicked in, and I could return to the former glory of doing my job well and having fun with the friends I'd made years before while doing it. Despite a bit of soreness, my hands handled the twelve hours perfectly fine.

After my first day back, I decided that working on lower-budget shows and commercials with people who I'd worked with previously and who I knew respected me was an excellent approach to returning to work. The last thing my body needed was the adrenalin-induced stress reaction to a Hollywood director I'd just met screaming at me if I made a mistake or didn't fulfill their requests fast enough.

This decision to surround myself with trusted peers allowed me to disclose my illness to producers and explain that I have a disability and may need help with physical tasks. To my surprise, I was met with compassion and have been on all but one production since. I ask for help on high pain days, and my peers are happy to assist me.

While I cannot predict what every job experience will be, when deciding which productions to take on next, I choose those that make me feel safe and do not strike me as hyper-reactive. More often than not, this means turning down long-term productions with people I've never worked with before, or occasionally the disappointing experience of turning down work with a team I love working with because it's too physically punishing, such as travelling to Pangnirtung or working deep in the forests of North Bay. Much like in a long-term relationship, I navigate my career based on trust. So far, this has worked in my favour. I'm happy to report that since January 2021, my arthritis has remained in remission.

In those two years after my diagnosis, I had to prioritize my health; I took advantage of my non-consensual downtime to pick up my pen and continue the writing projects floating about in my head that I'd never had the energy to tend to. While I appreciated the rest because it eased my stress, the physical act of writing changed for me due to my newfound relationship with pain. I prefer to write by hand on paper (or whatever I can find) with a black pen. Still, before reaching remission, I found the simple act of writing a sentence on the page was too much for the proximal interphalangeal joint in my right hand, where the pen applies pressure. Even typing on a keyboard sent searing pain through my joints. Sometimes, I wrote through it; other times, I cried or screamed.

The first year after a chronic illness diagnosis is often the most difficult in a patient's medical journey because it's a rollercoaster of an adjustment period where you find yourself tethered to the healthcare system with all of its procedures and flaws and new medications. What bothered me the most about my newfound dance with arthritis in my hands? The idea that one day I would lose my ability to write. That my hands would seize up into fists and never unclench again. Yes, I would be incapacitated and require a caregiver to eat and dress, which, admittedly, scared the shit out of me. But I wasn't there yet. In front of me were my blank pages and a new challenge: how to keep myself healthy and pain-free while also writing.

Eventually, I experimented with compression gloves; the thicker, the better. This allowed me to keep writing the way I was used to, with the smell of the ink reacting to the chemicals on the paper and reminding me that not everything has changed, not everything will be stolen from me. Once I accepted this, I was able to introduce new habits into my writing practice, including dictation.

Life looks and feels different now, but it isn't over. On low pain days, I am able to do something I loved despite the disease infiltrating my body. I believe this helped me heal and is one of the factors that directly contributed to my remission status.

While in the trenches of this new war with my bad biology, I established that one of my philosophies in life is that I will work to write. My creative endeavours became a priority, a necessary part of my existence, an entrenched facet of my identity that guided me through one of the lowest moments. I no longer work to keep up with the Joneses. Despite the time commitment of a nine-to-five being less than total hours on a film set, I find it overwhelming. I am not programmed to go to the same place every week for years at a time, minus two weeks of vacation.

Finding passion in my writing eroded my desire to make as much money as possible as quickly as possible. I will drive my rustbucket Chevy Impala into the ground and then buy used before I throw thirty grand at a new car—that adds up to six months of writing time! I don't need the latest iPhone. Or designer clothes. Or the hot tub I fantasize about but will (probably) never buy. Unless the money is for necessities such as my mortgage, food, and medical expenses, my health and writing are more important than anything money can buy. What I need to do is satiate that part of me that demands that I write!

I have conditioned myself to thrive on the unpredictability of the film industry, which now translates to my writing and chronically ill life. I create without knowing what tomorrow will look like and at a pace that I cannot predict. It is frustrating at times but beyond my control.

I believe that timing is everything, and that my creativity will have its time. I write whenever and wherever I can. In bursts when I feel it calling to me and occupying my thoughts until I relent and write it down. This idea started years ago when a fellow artist told me, "Set, we artists are like antennas, we receive a communication in the form of an idea. We don't get to know where the ideas come from, but when they come, we must pay attention because if we don't, they disappear or wander into the mind of another artist." This idea was articulated in Elizabeth Gilbert's *Big Magic*, when she discovered both she and Ann Patchett were writing essentially the same novel at the same time. "I believe inspiration will always try its best to work with you—but if you're not ready or available, it may indeed choose to leave you and to search for a different human collaborator."[1]

Whenever I think of something I want to remember and tell myself, *I'll remember it later*, I think of my friend telling me this and what happened to Elizabeth Gilbert. No matter where I am or what I'm doing, I find a way to get it down, even if it's a fragment I can use as a signpost later when I have time to develop the idea. Once illness infiltrated my life, this conviction applied to all of my creative work, not solely when a new idea popped into my head.

Finding comfort in the unpredictable is a challenge that takes practice—a writer must condition themselves to write anywhere and on anything. Write at work in moments of downtime: I've made a habit of writing and revising essays while watching files transfer on set. Write on your lunch break or on the toilet (or, in my case, the port-a-Johns at base camp for film crew). Write on the subway. Write on a cue card while waiting to pick up your kid from school. Write on napkins and sticky notes and on your phone and the back of the day's team meeting notes. I once wrote a line of dialogue for a horror movie with a Sharpie on my arm because I couldn't fumble with my notebook during a take of a feature film. Another time, I wrote a note on the centre console of my car while driving on the Trans-Canada Highway on my way to a job interview in Halifax. I do not recommend writing while operating heavy machinery despite my previous admission. Dictate it instead! Because you can't finish your masterpiece if you're dead.

The most significant contributor to my work-art-life balance is not conforming to the standard nine-to-five position, five days a week for fifty weeks out of the year. I only work when I have to or when the production that wants to hire me won't stress me to inflammation. I wish it didn't have to be this way, but this is how I've carved a life within my autoimmune disaster of an existence. This could mean a few commercials one month or a six-week television show with ten-hour capped days followed by a month off to rest. This balance depends on my physical and mental health, and if I have other deadlines I know I cannot meet while working.

It is impossible to pull off this never-ending balancing act if you are hard on yourself and hold yourself to punishing standards. It's a constant process of letting go of expectations while aspiring to live in the realm of work-art-life balance. I believe the idea of "balance" is a fallacy because life has its own agenda and doesn't adhere to even the most intricate planning a human can pull off. However, I aspire to it and keep this idea in the back of my mind when making any decision, whether it be life-related like a medication change, deciding whether to take a job, or whether I want to submit my work to a contest. I have never experienced the trifecta, where life, art, and work are equally tended to, and I likely never will. This is why it's best to be kind to oneself while being creative.

Instead of punishing yourself, get the ideas onto whatever medium you have at your disposal and then later put them into a document. Be flexible with yourself. Maybe that chapter you wanted to have done by the end of next week will take a few extra weeks because suddenly you're working twice as much to get a project out the door (maybe your project is children, that's valid, and my advice still applies). When I'm overworked, I avoid writing significant amounts or revising during periods of peak stress.

If I've learned anything from mutating into a chronically ill writer and filmmaker, self-care is of the utmost importance. This world isn't easy to live in, and we can't always do what we want when we want, especially if there are challenges such as disability. I take baby steps and do some of the not-so-glamorous but necessary work until I can lock myself away in a quiet space and put words to the page. As long as I keep putting in the work, I will get it done eventually. There is no use in wasting precious energy beating myself up about what I'm not getting done when I could be using it to revise that piece I'm dying to send out to my dream lit mag or composing a quick flash piece based on my unfinished manuscript. All efforts contribute to the greater body of work that is unique to ourselves.

When I first began my film career at twenty-two, I said yes to every job offer I was given to build my resumé and climb to a position where I could support myself financially. Once I got sick and experienced what it was to be incapacitated mid-career, I was forced to accept that this was no longer feasible for my body. This new perspective shifted my priorities to the point where, even though I can work again, I no longer have the instinct to work every day of the week and every week of the year. I know, I am a defective capitalist—a dysfunctional modern woman. Yet, refusing to work every day in the name of paper chasing helped my body heal and my mind rest into a zone where I can focus on a project and write. And since I'm no longer in agonizing pain every day, I can put in the work.

In our world, we are obligated to make money. This is the greatest burden of living in our time. The almighty dollar. It pays for every blouse, dinner, rent cheque, movie night, and birth control packet. But as an artist who is yearning to create art not in the name of someone else's vision, it's an endless chase.

As a creative in this industry, I know collaboration is a necessary part of the process to make any film, TV show, or commercial. Every person in every department has or once had the passion project they're funding with the money left over from their paycheques once the rent comes out. Those of us who aren't Canadian filmmaking royalty get their start volunteering on film sets or with low-paid positions like production assistants. These people climb to a job they enjoy, which may very well be their passion, but more often than not, even those with prestigious positions like director or cinematographer have projects of their own they would rather be working on. They are being paid to execute someone else's vision.

Since my career is in the artistic realm, another boundary I must enforce is distinguishing between my creative projects and those I'm hired to work on. The entertainment industry runs on collaboration, while writing is often quite solitary unless you're in a writer's room or have a writing partner. Knowing what I am doing on my own to feed the flames of my creative passions is essential so I don't get distracted. As John Cleese says, "The greatest killer to creativity is interruption."[2] I agree with this sentiment, and while I do my best to create despite work and life interruptions, I find the greatest interruption of all is being paid to work on someone else's art. This doesn't mean I don't strive to do the best job possible; in fact, I often do well enough that I'm offered more work at the end of my day. It's that I need a separation between the two realms of creativity, or my personal projects may suffer.

It is possible to be creative while working your ass off, even if your life is packed with challenges like time-vampire co-workers or a disabling illness. Knowing what you want to create and keeping it separate from what makes you money is challenging, especially when paid work makes up more than fifty percent of your waking time. But it's not impossible. Though I was able to carve out a new philosophy of work and creativity while incapacitated, this was a survival mechanism, not a place from which I could blast out the magical sentences found in a final draft. I learned that creativity is a process, and sometimes glacier-paced progress is necessary while finding balance and setting boundaries to take care of ourselves.

I no longer put myself in a position to be overworked or overbooked. I guard my schedule depending on my health and writing needs. There are times when I cannot book time to write due to my capitalistic responsibilities. Instead, I must accept what I can do, even if it's only a sentence. I used to live boundary-free, and my creativity floundered. Now I am more creatively fulfilled and productive than I have ever been.

It's just after 3:00 AM, and I'm lying in bed. My partner and cat are snoring beside me. The room is pitch black but for flashes of lightning from a summer storm outside my window. I pick up my phone and read an email that's just come in. A stranger is asking for my availability for a feature film next month. I squeeze my left hand into a fist as I have countless times a day ever since my diagnosis. There's no pain. Only a familiar stiffness that comes with the territory of being an RA patient.

I place my phone face down on my bedside table and lie back, thinking about who I know that can take on this job instead of me. I'm tired and need rest. A few names come to mind.

The next day, I email back, letting them know I am not available and recommending two others who might take my place. They get back to me almost immediately, thanking me and wishing me well.

When that feature goes to camera the next month, I sit at home writing a chapter of my memoir. I couldn't be happier.

Author's Note: I wrote this essay almost entirely under non-ideal conditions: while working twelve hours a day on the sets of five commercials and one television show. This was written on my phone, in my notebook, on bar napkins, and on the backs of discarded camera reports.

You should know that this essay was composed before the 2023 WGA and SAG strikes, which brought the North American entertainment industry to a standstill, putting tens of thousands of crew out of work, including myself. I lost all of my savings, but got a hell of a lot of writing done between panic attacks.

SET L. SHUTER is a writer, filmmaker, and storyteller from Toronto. She's a graduate of The Humber School for Writers and holds an MFA in Creative Nonfiction from The University of King's College. Her literary work has appeared in *Understorey Magazine, Creative Nonfiction Magazine, Chatelaine, The Toronto Star,* CBC and more. Her short film *What's Killing Lilith?* is based on her experiences with chronic illness outlined in her memoir-in-progress, *Autoimmune Disaster,* and is playing at film festivals across North America. When she isn't on stage or working, you can find her watching a horror movie in the dark or in Nova Scotia, writing her days away by the ocean.

No Magic Formula

I often get asked a version of the same question: Do you ever sleep?

I actually get plenty of sleep, but I have an inkling about why people ask. I have a high output at times, but no one sees the messy part of the process, only the product. That I procrastinate and work on several projects at a time, or that I leave as many projects unfinished as finished, is unseen. I have a monkey mind. I multi-task many projects most of the time, but I am also highly skilled in procrastination. I nest. I organize my supplies, research ideas, clean my house, wipe countertops frequently—anything but create!

Allowing multiple external pressures to take away time I set aside to create serves as a procrastination device as well. I prioritize work for others, like editing, marking papers, or reviewing minutes for a meeting—all of which usurp time for creativity. I also don't give myself any margin around my commitments or tasks, but I somehow still manage to have outputs that I am satisfied with. I don't often just sit. I try to squeeze as much as possible out of each day—to be efficient with my time—always.

At first this question about my sleep—and its implications about my productivity—bothered me. I felt hypocritical or like an imposter for some reason, but it prompted me to think about creativity, time, process, and product a great deal. I felt compelled to understand my productivity because I didn't think what I did was that unusual or different from others. I thought perhaps if I could figure that out it might be of benefit to other creatives.

I have been creative most of my life—engaging in knitting, photography, painting, needlework, sewing, and embroidery. I seemed to always be working on something. But, during the peak of my career-building years, I let much of that go. I was married and had a demanding business. I felt I didn't have the time to maintain my creative endeavours, so I simply stopped doing my artistic projects—every single one. I worked long hours, built programs, sat on boards and committees related to my work, solved problems, drafted briefing notes, and did a lot of public speaking—either to promote our family business or for paying gigs as a featured speaker at events and conferences. Because some of those things were creative by nature, they fed my soul and need for creative work, namely imagining and developing programs, and drafting the talks and workshops I offer. Yet, those things didn't offer the same experience as creating for the enjoyment of producing something beautiful.

A year after my son was born, I began my PhD. Working part-time and studying required me to do less of what I wanted to do, and do more of what I *had* to do. With multiple pressures on my time, I wasn't living a fully balanced life, but I nurtured my need for creativity through the cooking and baking that sprang out of the necessity to eat. During my PhD studies, I spent more time writing than any other time in my life. While writing can be creative, it isn't often the case when it comes to academic papers with rules to follow, as in assignments or submitting a scholarly paper to a journal.

In my second or third year, I attended Women's Words, an enriching week-long series of writing workshops. One workshop I participated in was art journaling. The main takeaway from the instructor literally changed my outlook: *create or be sick*. As I listened to her, I knew without a doubt, that what she said was true.

At the time, I was entrenched in the academic world with studying and researching consuming most of my waking moments, leaving time for little else. It had to be that way to excel in my studies, but I could take baby steps back to nourishing my creative needs. At the time, I was often overwhelmed by the pressures of school and work where I had a leadership role. Various demands allowed me little control over how I spent my time, facing deadline after deadline. I also had a young son, a home to run, and thankfully a very supportive husband. I was doing little to nurture my creativity. I recognized myself, then, when that art journaling teacher said *create or be sick.* The workshop was nourishing to my soul. I knew it was time to bring more intentional creativity back into my life.

It doesn't necessarily matter what you create, as long as you have a creative outlet that is meaningful for you. *Create or be sick* was my way of appreciating that, in order to be fully content, I had to exercise and nurture my creative as well as my analytic nature. I began practising more creative writing in addition to the required academic writing. For example, I came across a book for qualitative researchers using creative exercises to stretch your brain. One of the exercises was to use haiku in analyzing my research. It stimulated not only other ways of looking at my data, and generated poetry, but those seventeen-syllable haiku took me down a rabbit hole. I immediately saw where I could use different creative mediums to enhance data analysis and analytical thinking, and where I could apply different media to stimulate different thinking and problem solving in other areas of my life.

I began studying and applying arts-based methods in not only my research, but also my teaching, writing, and nearly every aspect of my work and productivity. Using multiple media, I found a way to bring more creative aspects to what is often seen as the antithesis of creative thinking—analytic thinking. I felt more alive and whole than I had in a long time. The more I exercised my creative brain, the better my analytic brain worked. The more fully

I was able to bring creative aspects into my life, rather than using creativity only as a means to an end, it became a much bigger part of my life. I felt more whole. I loved the process as much as the product, and I embraced the messiness of it. Arts-based and creative outlets nurtured me to the end of my PhD and became part of my whole approach to teaching and learning as a professor. *Create or be sick* has become a phrase I often use when nurturing creativity both in myself and in others.

Over time, I found my way back to my creative roots in textile arts, making jewellery as well as maintaining a creative writing practice. By revelling in the process as much as the product, I noticed I was using many different mediums. I had several different artistic pursuits on the go at a time, in my work and leisure time. However, sometimes I become overwhelmed with too much— too much stuff, too many ideas, too many projects. When overwhelmed, I procrastinate. I've learned that procrastination is how I slow down and cope, but it also made me question how I let the cycle of overwhelm happen in the first place.

I jump in with both feet when I learn something new, so that means studying the history and form, practising the techniques, and purchasing tools, books, and supplies to fully develop my newfound endeavours. As I moved from one project to the next, I noticed I liked some things more than others. But, the overwhelm had to be managed. Recognizing overwhelm, I realized it was time to pare down, to declutter both my space and my mind and let things go in order to move forward. This was also about the time I began to notice how often I got the questions about my sleep habits. I took a deeper dive into thinking about my productivity, periods of overwhelm, and how and when overwhelm happens. It led me to question what motivates my creativity in the first place. I contemplated what motivates me in two ways: intentionally at specific times, but also by letting the question steep in my thoughts on a more subconscious level. While the question about my sleep may have been the initial prompt, it was my regular yoga practice that gave me the space to more deeply contemplate the question of motivation.

I started practising yoga a few years prior, and like many who are new to yoga I was most interested in its physical benefits. As I learned to meditate better and embrace the mind-body connection, I noticed my mental acuity was changing. Although I was knowledgeable about the theoretical aspects of the mind-body connection, it became embodied through my yoga practice. I noticed how the mind-body awareness brought my attention into sharper focus over time. It is hard to describe what happens in meditation as many of the benefits are not noticed initially. There are many degrees and stages happening at a subconscious level. Meditation experts might not agree with my descriptors or experience, and that's okay. This was my experience with embodied knowing through meditation rather than expert advice.

I have a monkey mind as I stated earlier. It needs to be tamed and meditation helped the chatter settle. Meditation felt like hard work and, like learning anything, to be good at meditation you have to practise. I am not sure exactly how long it was, but after about six to twelve months, I was beginning to be able to still my mind, be comfortable in a lying or seated position, and fully embrace the benefits of savasana* or longer periods of meditation. I noticed that, when I came back to awareness after a guided meditation, savasana, or other meditative practice, I would have the spark of an idea or the answer to a question I was not necessarily aware I needed. I started to dream up a new design, or a new story to write, or a new way to solve a problem. I worked at reigning in my monkey mind. Once I was able to slow my mind, greater clarity would come with ideas, designs, and solutions.

Once I started to focus on what motivated me and paid attention to my creative practice, the answer came reasonably quick. I

---

* The final resting pose at the end of a yoga session.

am motivated by learning and mastering new things—new skills, new techniques, or exploring whole new fields or artforms. This knowledge was freedom. It gave me permission to embrace all that motivated and inspired me and to let go of the rest. It gave me clarity and the drive to pare down all of the clutter in my mind and studio. I became comfortable letting go of all the things and forms that I didn't love, only keeping those that served me and knowing that I would embrace new media, techniques, and artforms in the future.

I was able to get into my own flow with the artistic process, whether it was writing, working with fibre, sewing, anything. If I didn't love a particular medium or activity, if I struggled to stay in a flow, or if I wasn't feeling some sense of joy, I could easily let go and shift the aspects that weren't working, or quit the project entirely. I find it difficult to quit anything, in part due to my relentless drive to succeed, so being able to let go without remorse, regret, or angst was a huge hurdle. It was easier to overcome this through understanding and embracing what motivates me— understanding my why. Learning what motivates my creative needs and process was like a light bulb that went off, and it freed up my time, my space, and my mind of clutter.

I also don't seem to procrastinate quite as often. I still do, but I don't do it because of overwhelm anymore. I don't care what my process looks like, because I understand it. I am not as suspicious of myself, nor do I feel like an imposter. Time is finite, and I still pack as much into any given day as I can. I still tend to err on the side of meeting commitments to others first, like editing for someone or teaching, and that pilfers time from my own creative pursuits, but I do it much less often. I am better at prioritizing my own creative pursuits.

While most of us need to prioritize time for family, work, and school responsibilities, it is not necessarily okay to always do so at the expense of our own creative needs. It is not selfish to create or nurture our creative selves. Through acknowledging what motivates me and recognizing my basic need to create, I learned to choose better. During times of particular busyness, I have to carve out time to create; to make it a priority as well. How to find the time to create is different for everyone. For me, it varies and depends on how much I procrastinate and what deadlines are imposed. Sometimes, first thing in the morning is best for me to write, and I push back other work until I have met my writing goal for the day. Other times I take a whole day—usually on the weekend—to create uninterrupted, usually a textile product or when I want to make a lot of headway on a piece of writing. And sometimes taking a whole day on a project is necessary because I procrastinated so long that I have no choice! I try to pay attention to what is on my to-do list, especially items I can complete in short order, and defer doing them outside of the time when I know I do my best work and where my higher energy is better spent on a bigger project of my own choosing.

On a regular basis, I do prepared or finite tasks in the evening while watching a movie with my husband like hand-stitching or embellishing a garment. For me, there is something sacred about saying no to everything else for a block of time so I can create uninterrupted. So, while I chose to stay in my studio to play for an hour or two after my regular (paid or volunteer) work commitments are done, or take a half-day off from studying and research to create, that might not work for others. It's a choice we all make: how to spend our time. We all have a finite amount and unique pressures specific to our lives.

I value a regular schedule for sleep and family mealtimes so those things in my day are rarely sacrificed. I say *rarely* because if I have to meet a deadline for a farmers' market or I want to complete some new designs, I might make a short-term sacrifice, but it isn't a usual thing.

Balance ebbs and flows like the rest of life, and nurturing our mental and physical health and our relationships cannot be ignored. There is no magic formula, no right or wrong way, no routine that lasts forever. It was learning to balance my need to create in the middle of other demands and pressures that gave me freedom to create. While I may not have a regular schedule every day, I can create a rhythm to my day.

I was only able to embrace *my process* after learning what motivated me—learning and mastering. But then I had to explore that a bit. What is enough? Mastery of anything takes years of practise, and hours and hours of investment. I certainly didn't do that with most of my pursuits. I had to find out what was enough for me. There were things I tried that never stuck with me, or that I knew I wouldn't go back to. Knowing I am motivated by learning new things, and that often my intent in creating something, whether a piece of writing or a product, is mastering it to a degree that I am happy with allows me to move on. That knowledge has worked well for me because it lets me move beyond the burden of holding onto what isn't serving me.

For some things, it was just knowing how to do it; for others, like making jewellery, it was enough to make something well. In the case of writing, it is to get as close to my voice as possible. Some things, like writing, take me way longer than others, like making jewellery, collaging a story, or sewing something by machine or hand. These are my current loves. And, I also learned that what I do with my hands helps me with what I think in my head.

Changing gears to feed both *doing* and *thinking* are necessary for *my process*. If I can't find a way through a storyline, I stop and make something with my hands. Through the repetitive, quiet meditation of making something tactile, I think in an unplanned way. I am quieting my mind, and this quieting allows the answers to come. Through the cycle of making, doing, and thinking, I thrive.

It took me a while to understand my creative cycle and my ideal conditions for creativity. I write more now, but not nearly as much as I'd like. I don't submit much for publication, but I should. I still procrastinate, but I set goals and use my timer, and that helps— like when doing my edits for this essay! Other things are calling me. I want to cut out a dress pattern I have laid out; I am in the middle of sewing a cute summer top; I am embroidering a design on a denim vest; and I want to clean up my stash of embroidery threads because I bought a new storage bin for them. My monkey mind still needs constant taming. But this is the deadline in front of me, so I set my timer to work on this for seventy-five minutes. Realizing I can always add ten or twenty minutes to my timer helps me be productive, knowing my reward is playing with my fabrics. Setting conditions around various tasks helps me accomplish a lot more.

Although I currently have several projects on the go, I embrace the messiness inherent in the idea stage of getting things down, creating my piles for each project, and having an area set aside where I can actually do the work of creating. When I get down to the work of refining and finishing, I have to use strategies to focus on a single project for a short time, like my timer and a reward. My high output isn't always pretty, but I don't worry about pretty in my process anymore.

For me, multiple projects, my creative monkey mind, and the time factor somehow work in sync and keep me thriving as a maker. I *need* several things on the go because I need to tap into my own rhythm of creating. The more I have on the go, the easier I get into flow with each project. Being in flow on one project is meditative for me, and when that magic happens, solutions to challenges I have on other projects often come to mind. The seed of understanding this process is related to accepting the bad artist in me—the multiple projects, the messiness of my process, and procrastination. This leads to a greater return on my time investment than only doing one project at a time. Again, it wasn't until I understood what motivated me—prompted by questions about my sleep habits—that I was able to appreciate the natural limits of my time and achieve my deepest desires. I stress that this is what works *for me*; intrinsic motivators vary, and I appreciate that my tactics won't work for everyone.

In my experience, time and creativity have an inverse relationship: that is, less is often more in the midst of everything else. Not to negate the fact that a regular day job, or any paying gig, and family or social commitments create time factors that aren't easily negotiated. The answer lies within the space we can often manipulate to use time in creative ways. It varies for all of us.

I've attempted an honest portrayal of how I tame my inner bad artist. I never do one thing at a time—ever. I don't recall a time that I ever did. I multi-task, and this is usually controlled using the tools I mentioned: understanding my motivations and creative needs, using my timer, and giving myself rewards. When my multi-tasking isn't managed, I am all over the place. Procrastination can seep in and stall me. When I get to the stage in any creative project that requires deep focus and concentration, I'm single-minded. I focus on the task at hand for a dedicated amount of time using my timer. I can set it again, but I am reminded of the task at hand when it goes off and can make a choice: keep going or switch gears. I am not a superhuman creator, and I do sleep for seven to eight hours a night! In spite of my procrastination, I have learned to be aware of where and how I spend my time.

KIM FRASER, PhD, MFA, MA (Health Education), RN, is a nursing professor and a creative with a focus on mixed fibre art, restyling/upcycling clothing, quilting, jewellery-making, and writing. Yoga keeps her sane and healthy.

The Lemurs Make Me Write

Although I do not wear a white lab coat, don protective glasses, or work with chemicals in test tubes, I am a scientist.

Channelling my inner Jane Goodall, I spent fourteen months living and working in Madagascar—the Alberta-sized island off the southeast coast of Africa. I travelled to the northwest of the country to study lemurs, the most endangered group of animals on the planet, in their natural habitat and contribute to their conservation. Members of the species I studied, the Coquerel's sifaka, are snowy-white with maroon patches of fur on their arms and legs that make them look like they are wearing overcoats and trousers, like distinguished professors. Using their long, powerful hindlimbs, these lemurs propel themselves in great leaps from tree to tree, crossing ten-metre gaps in a single bound. My job as a scientific researcher was to find these lemurs and follow them through the forest from dawn to dusk, recording information about what they did, where they went, and what they ate.

Although I do not wear a beret or carry a palette peppered with vibrant acrylic blotches of paint, I am an artist.

My medium is the written word. I write short stories, full-length books, fiction, and nonfiction; nothing is off limits. After graduating with my PhD, I opened my creative floodgates. Inspired by the incredible biodiversity in Madagascar, which sadly faces a conservation crisis, I took to the page but surprised myself when what came out was creative rather than academic. I have since realized that my scientific background shapes my art and that its influence on my artistic practice goes beyond the subject matter.

Discipline.

Observation.

Innovative approaches.

Resilience in the face of setbacks.

Each of the attributes I developed as a scientist plays an important role in my approach to writing.

5:00 AM, wake up.

My Timex digital watch chirps, and I blink awake. It takes me a moment to realize where I am. I blink again, and the tent poles come into focus above my head. I shift in my sleeping bag and hear the familiar squeak of my Thermarest mattress beneath me. I take a deep breath, and the crisp morning air fills my lungs.

Here we go again.

Sitting up, I hear the call of the sickle-billed vanga, my favourite bird. Like much of the Madagascar wildlife, this bird is found only on the island of Madagascar and nowhere else on the planet. Black and white with a long, curved bill, the vanga sounds eerily like a baby crying.

Waaa, waaa!

The forest is waking.

I shimmy into my field uniform, which I have laid next to my sleeping bag—long, quick-dry pants and a button-down, quick-dry shirt. I unzip my three-person tent—my nylon sanctuary—and crawl out on my hands and knees. The night before, I placed my hiking boots at the door of my tent. I pick up my boots one at a time, give them a shake and bang them against the post of my tent platform—an important step to oust any scorpions or other insects that may have found a new home overnight.

I am quiet and careful where I shine my headlamp; I do not want to wake the others. I live in a research camp, the sole Canadian among teams from Japan, Germany, and South Africa. The camp is situated in northwest Madagascar, in Ankarafantsika National Park, home to eight different lemur species living in one of Madagascar's last protected dry forests.

I find my research assistant, a slim, soft-spoken Malagasy university student named Lanto, waiting outside his tent. The two of us will grab a quick breakfast of rice, some meat, and most importantly, coffee.

"Are you ready?" I whisper to Lanto.

It is time to head to the forest.

5:00 AM, rise-and-shine.

My Apple watch buzzes, and I blink into consciousness. The stucco ceiling above me comes into focus—the air conditioner whirs. My partner, Travis, turns over in the bed as I quietly rise and open the door, careful not to make a sound.

I continued my 5:00 AM wake-up time after returning from field research. At first, I blamed it on the jet lag, but now, in my Ontario home, mornings have become my writing time—the time before the rest of the world awakes. Before I feel myself pulled in many directions—my day job, house chores, family obligations.

In our washroom, I splash cold water on my face. I look in the mirror, analyzing the freckles I developed from the hours I spent in the sun looking for lemurs.

"You're ready," I whisper to my reflection.

I slip on my hoodie, which I have left hanging on the washroom door. I pick up my slippers from the landing of the staircase. I stop, smiling a little as I remember there is no need to shake these out. No scorpions here—at least, I hope!

Quietly, I make my way downstairs. It is still dark out, but I don't mind. It feels cozy. In the kitchen, I place my French press

onto the kitchen scale and slowly measure out my coffee. I start
the kettle and pour half-and-half into my favourite mug.

It is time to fill that blank page.

Searching for Lemurs

When I embarked on my career as a primatologist, I never guessed
that finding the lemurs would be the most difficult of all my tasks.
Many primatologist colleagues used radio collars—small, black
plastic collars equipped with radio transmitters—to track the individuals and groups they studied. For the German researchers
studying the aptly named mouse lemur—so small it could fit inside a teacup—affixing the collars was not such a big deal. They
would set out small metal live traps, bait them with bananas, and
then bring the mouse lemurs back to camp, where they would
put on the collars and weigh and measure them. But those mouse
lemurs weighed a mere sixty grams. The lemurs I studied were
eight kilograms. Sure, capturing and putting collars on them was
possible, but it would have been much more invasive. I had seen
it done. A researcher shoots the lemur in the tree with an anaes-
thetic dart and waits until the creature falls asleep. The lemur then
tumbles from the tree while a team below holds out a blanket,
hoping to catch the falling lemur.

I opted not to put the lemurs through that and instead relied
on human skill to find them each morning. With my Malagasy research assistant, Lanto, and forest guide, Zama, I would head out
each morning before sunrise. We would split up once we hit the
forest trails, each carrying a walkie-talkie.

"You take the main trail while I check out that fruiting tree," I
would say before we split.

We got to know the trees the lemurs liked—large trees they
could sleep in and that held fruit at certain times of the year.

After we split up, each of us walked the trail slowly. We used
all our senses. We scanned the forest canopy above our heads for

a glimpse of white fur and listened for the familiar rustle of leaves. Then there was the smell. If the lemurs had just left an area, they would leave behind a pungent, botanical odour characteristic of a leaf-eating primate.

Some mornings, we found the lemurs immediately.

"Keriann," Lanto's voice would come through on the radio. "*Ils sont ici.*"

On those days, I would breathe a sigh of relief.

But other days, we would need an hour or two to find the group we were chasing. That was okay. We had a strategy—split up and search the trails. Keep going. It wasn't easy, but usually, it got the job done. We would find the group and begin data collection.

Then there were the toughest days—the days we would walk in circles along the trails, the three of us scouring the forest canopy for hours, hiking and walking. Some days, after spending five or six hours going in circles, we turned up nothing and would return to camp empty-handed.

Try again tomorrow.

Searching for Story

Maybe it was the time I spent walking in circles looking for lemurs, but now I don't take for granted that writing will come easy. Some mornings it will; I'll hit that deep concentration and calm as the words pour out of me—that creative flow. That feeling is what gets me out of bed in the morning. My head buzzes, and I feel an energy in my chest as I visualize the letters. The letters swirl around me, and I can see them form words in my mind's eye. The words come together in sentences. Just like that, the story is at my fingertips.

Those days, I am a real writer.

Then there are the other days. The days when the words don't come. The days when writing feels like work. It is so easy to let my mind wander. Round and round in circles.

I must add eggs to my grocery list—don't forget the eggs.

You didn't get your workout in yesterday.

Oh, that email! That important work email!

I close my eyes and try to visualize the letters, words, and sentences, but like a word search, it is just a jumble.

I try typing, but all that comes out are sentence fragments—beginnings of ideas that, as quickly as they emerge, melt away into nothingness like the icicles on my window.

The ice! I must put down the salt on the walkway!

I stare at the computer screen, and the imposter syndrome hits hard.

Who am I to call myself a writer?

Then I remember the lemurs. When I cannot find what I am looking for, I remind myself that I don't quit.

Maybe I spend that morning mapping out the structure of what I am about to write—honing my outline or moving pieces around to find the flow. Perhaps I will work on something new. Something just for fun.

My fieldwork with the lemurs taught me persistence and that there will always be tough days—when, no matter what I try, I come up empty and can't find the story.

As I did chasing lemurs, I persist.

I will try again tomorrow.

Scientific Observations

Rocky was one of my favourite lemurs. He was a large male who belonged to a group of seven—three females, two males, and a couple of juveniles. But Rocky was not always Rocky. He earned his name two months into my study.

It was a sunny morning, and we quickly found the group I had been diligently following, collecting behavioural samples.

Scientific observation is a skill. While I followed the group around for twelve hours a day like a weirdo stalker, I also conducted "focal-animal samples," where I would focus on one of the individual lemurs for ten-minute periods. Armed with my digital watch and a data sheet affixed to a clipboard, I'd write down every behaviour an individual did during those ten minutes.

That morning had been relatively quiet. The lemurs had been moving around and feeding, but so far, nothing out of the ordinary had happened. Then at about ten in the morning, while I watched one of the females resting, a skirmish broke out between the two males. It was epic. I knew from my training that the best thing to do during a series of unusual behaviours is to abandon the formal sampling protocol and write down everything about what you observe. Such are the methods Jane Goodall used with the chimpanzees.

The fight lasted a few minutes. It reminded me of a cartoon Tasmanian devil—a spinning ball of lemurs above me in the forest canopy. They moved from the tree to the ground and then back again. High-pitched chirps emanated from the lemur ball. Then, abruptly, other members of the group bolted hither and yon. The males went one way, the females with the young lemurs another.

Lanto and I split up, each trying to stick with half the group, but I soon lost sight of the males, who could cover ten metres through the canopy in a single leap. And now they were moving fast.

Ultimately, only one of the males returned. For weeks, the group was down to six individuals. One of the males had disappeared. I wondered if he had been killed or chased away, never to return.

About a month later, as I stood watching the lemurs feed one afternoon, a large male lemur approached along some low branches. I could see he had been in a skirmish, with a torn ear and scars on his face. All at once, I realized—it was him! The male that had been chased away from the group had returned. Like Rocky Balboa, this lemur might have been down, but he was not out. He rejoined the group as though nothing had happened.

This event and Rocky are burned into my memory, and I know it is because I truly observed. I kept careful notes. I noted the tiny details and the significant events—I was thorough and consistent. I documented everything.

Artistic Observations

When I returned from Madagascar, I could not help but observe primates of the human variety. I began noticing more details in my everyday world. I saw the merry way my mail delivery woman walked as though she had just received a piece of good news. I listened as the two women seated behind me on the bus discussed their problem with a colleague. The woman with the high-pitched, nasal voice marked the end of her sentences with a question mark.

At first, I thought of this observation skill as nothing more than a party trick. Sure, I would watch how my colleague scraped her teeth against her fork with every bite of food in the cafeteria, but how could I possibly put this skill to use?

Then I found creative writing. I learned that noticing the small things is a writing technique. Golden details, they're called. I carry a small notebook everywhere, just like I did during my scientific fieldwork. In it, I jot down what I observe.

Of course, there are days when I am stressed or distracted—when I spend too much time on my phone—and I forget to note those golden details. The distractions are why I carry the notebook. It serves as a tangible reminder. When I am digging around for my house keys and feel the coils of that spiral-bound book, I momentarily transport back to the forest and into the mindset I developed—the months I spent filling the pages of my notebook with observations. Channelling that mindset has immense value in my creative work.

The blond woman with the scab on her knee I saw at the dog park?

I put her into the short story I am writing.

The detail about how my father goes quiet when he thinks something over?

I used that in my memoir.

Observing and capturing the golden details—as I did with the lemurs—makes me a better writer.

Developing Resilience

In fieldwork, with the magical comes the maddening. Although my job was to find and follow one lemur species, there was much more to observe in the forest. There were eight different species of lemur—each of them with unique quirks. Some were active during the day, some at night. Some ranged around the forests in solitary groups, while others lived in groups of a dozen or more. Beyond the lemurs, the forest was home to colourful chameleons, boas and leaf snakes, countless colourful birds and even large, hairy bush pigs. I was treated to wildlife sightings daily on my morning "commute" to find lemurs. I could not believe my luck, living amongst the forest creatures in a real-life Garden of Eden.

But I encountered challenges too. Although the forest where I worked is considered dry, I quickly learned that dry forests are not always dry. The rainy season runs from November through April. Oh, and around February, the cyclones pass through. There were weeks when we didn't see the sun. Our field equipment and tent grew patches of white mould. We ran out of dry socks. Yet, the data collection had to go on. I persevered through the rains because I had to. I tapped into resilience that I did not know I had.

Then there were health issues. In Madagascar, contaminated food or water often causes illness. Madagascar is sadly one of the poorest countries in the world, with many people living on less than two dollars a day. While I would bounce back from the various bouts of food-induced diarrhea, I knew that many people in the surrounding communities where I worked suffered daily.

Malaria is also a real risk. A year into my PhD program, I soon discovered what "the worst" can look like. Along with my PhD supervisor, I travelled to Kasijy Special Reserve—a remote wilderness site thirty kilometres from the nearest village in the northwest of Madagascar. On that journey, I experienced food poisoning, impassable backcountry roads, complicated local politics, and a gruelling hike along sandy shores and across raging rivers. Our team made it to an idyllic forested field site where the lemurs were abundant—practically dropping out of the trees—and started to collect data. My PhD supervisor departed, leaving me in charge. A few days after my supervisor left, my field assistant, a university student named Andry—and the only person with me who spoke English or French—contracted malaria. It was up to me to bring him to safety. So, left with no other options, I coordinated an emergency evacuation using my broken Malagasy, transporting Andry by dugout canoe and makeshift stretcher to the village where he could receive treatment.

Andry recovered, but we could not return to Kasijy. I spent the rest of my time in Madagascar searching for a new field site that was easy to access, where I could safely study the lemurs.

I credit that experience with teaching me important life skills. Channelling grit, I brought Andry to safety. Mustering determination, I found a new place to work—Ankarafantsika. I returned to Madagascar with resolve, where I would live in a tent and study the lemurs for fourteen months straight.

Channelling Resilience

Practising science in Madagascar changed my perspective and worldview.

Writing and trying to publish is not easy. I submit my stories and manuscripts, and I receive rejection letters. I apply for grants, spending hours developing my application materials, only to receive a form email directing me to the grant results where I see the word unsuccessful, and my heart drops.

But if field research taught me anything, persistence pays off. I revise and resubmit my stories and pitches. I modify my grant applications and try again. This resilience pays off—when my work is accepted or if I win a grant, I am hit with a rush of excitement and am ready to keep writing every day.

The biggest lesson I took from my experience as a scientific researcher has been one of priorities. Through my struggles—and seeing the struggles of so many of the Malagasy people I got to know—I realized that health and wellness trump everything else. When life feels hard, I think about Andry and how he shivered uncontrollably in his tent in the throes of his malaria fever. I think about how nothing else—not even the scientific data I was collecting—mattered more than getting him to safety immediately. I think about the people in the communities in Madagascar who are living hand to mouth. I think about how what matters above all is that they can feed their families and stay healthy.

I feel incredibly privileged that I can write—that I am healthy, have food to eat and a roof over my head. When I write, I recognize my privilege. And I try to write with purpose.

I am a scientist who does art—an artist who knows science. I navigate my way through a story as I did through the forest. I persist when I face rejection and develop a routine during times of uncertainty. I observe. I focus. I discover.

KERIANN MCGOOGAN is an English major turned primatologist turned author. In pursuit of primates, she has kayaked Central American rivers, waded through seasonally flooded forests, and contended with disturbingly large mosquito populations. Her memoir, *Chasing Lemurs: My Journey into the Heart of Madagascar*, was published in 2020 by Prometheus Books. Her writing has also appeared in *The Nashwaak Review*, the *Toronto Star*, *Outpost Magazine*, *Verge Magazine*, and *Wanderlust Magazine*. In 2021, Keriann was selected as a Writers' Trust Rising Star.

Field Notes on Patience (in Shreds)

Patience Out There

Most definitions of *patience* have a whiff of martyrdom to them. Here's one from the Oxford Dictionary: "the ability to stay calm and accept a delay or something annoying without complaining."

In the last century, Axl Rose of the four-octave pipes sang a tender song about patience. In the video, images dissolve—a hotel hallway, a woman in and out of bed, a snake. Finally, a man enters a hotel room where the bedside phone is flashing a message. As Rose croons "need a little patience," the man hurls the phone set to the floor and stomps on it until pieces fly apart. Fun fact: the Guns N' Roses singer is known for keeping live audiences waiting for over an hour.

The other day a truck driver rode my bumper for a kilometre or so, then roared past me only to meet me at the red light. This happens often, and I'm not a slow driver. I was about to wave at him, but he was looking straight ahead.

Relax, she probably hasn't read your email. It's Tuesday and you only sent it Friday. She's busy. She has a life-threatening illness. She's read it and because you never activated "read receipt" on your email you will never know (what kind of control freak activates "read receipt" anyway? You're not a lawyer). She's already read it and finds it so terrible she is stalling in order to find the words to tell you that. She's read it, but since you told her that you were going away for a week she's assuming you're not checking your email and it can wait. You can wait. Tell yourself you can wait. Start another project, weed the garden, go for a walk. Read a book. She's busy. You don't always answer other people's emails within a day or so, so why should she? She has a life. You have a life. What is she doing? Check her social media. What is she doing?

No surprise, but few female babies are named Patience anymore. It's a name I associate with rosy-cheeked English girls wearing pinafores and shiny black Mary Janes. In the 1600s the Puritans began to give female children the name, perhaps to inspire this virtue in the child. Patience and Prudence were a sister group famous in the last century for songs like "Tonight You Belong to Me" and "Gonna Get Along Without Ya Now." At the ages of eleven and fourteen, they sang songs for adults while trying to live up to their names. I mean, aren't Faith and Hope difficult enough?

Flashbulb memory. Shortly after a death in the family, I entered the university seminar room to be swarmed by students wanting answers to x, y, or z. All were giving presentations that day and, to my mind, were needlessly fraught. It was early in my teaching career and I hadn't encountered such unbridled panic from adults before. Surely, they knew I was flexible. The force of a dozen panicked voices hit me like a wave, and I snapped. The room went silent. People took to their seats and scowled. I still feel guilty about it.

"Talent is long patience." Gustav Flaubert.
"Rivers know this. There is no hurry. We shall get there some day." A. A. Milne.
"Patience is a conquering virtue." Geoffrey Chaucer.
"Patience, Grasshopper." Master Po.
Easy for them to say, right?

Obviously, the boy was too young for this. The animals were nine hundred to one thousand kilograms and together created a force that could crush him like a grape. They turned away from him as he flailed his goad, trying and failing to move them forward. Their eyes flashed. The stone boat carried two one-hundred-kilogram concrete slabs, and each time the team pulled the sled sideways or lurched ahead too quickly, the boy jumped around them, shrieking and striking the animals. Other teamsters in the ox pull led their teams with calm voices and steady movements. The boy's oxen didn't score well enough to continue. He became angry and frustrated and the men around him patted his back and shook his hand. Later I learned it can take four years of persistence and steady patience to train an ox to trust its handler.

Hang on. Who is expected to be patient? As a woman, I have been trained since childhood not to complain. To stay calm. To endure. Door-pounding and fist-shaking outrage has never been my style. If it were, I'd be labelled hysterical, hormonal, and, well, a threat. Worse, if I had darker skin and showed any kind of impatience at all, I'd likely be in grave danger.

Only some people seem to be given a pass for yelling at cashiers, stomping on phones, slamming doors, driving aggressively, shooting off snarky remarks, and being cruel to animals. My father was always in high dudgeon about something: a mistake on the heating bill, a flaw in a purchase, the wait to be seated in a restaurant. I'll never know if his outbursts resulted in better service, but I doubt it. I deal with my impatience using the squeaky wheel approach. As I paced the emergency room recently, my blood pressure at stroke level and climbing, I kept calm as I continued to approach the triage nurse to ask when I'd be seen. Again. And again. I could have died from the kind of patience I've learned to display. But I could have died throwing a tantrum, too.

What's hardly worth our annoyance and what threatens our survival? We wait while the elderly gentlemen at the post office futzes over labelling four packages and complains to the clerk about "service these days." We grit our teeth as we are stonewalled for six months by a literary journal. Should we turn the other cheek when landlords repeatedly refuse to show us an apartment if we are new to the country? How much patience did Carol Shields have when her novels were consistently criticized for their domesticity? Does that require mere patience, or something else entirely?

Other words for patience:

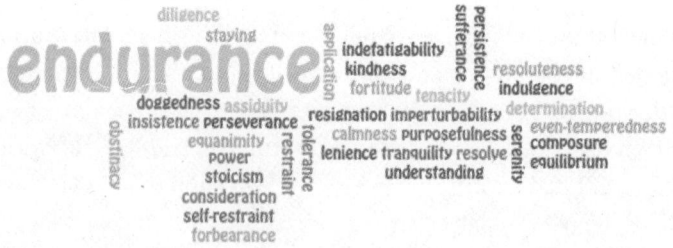

Lessons in Patience

Finally, I have a quiet morning, and I'm deep in thought about an approach to an essay when I hear a knock at the back door. I guess a closed curtain isn't signal enough.

"Hi, I won't stay," calls my neighbour in his outside voice as he steps past me into the kitchen and begins to tell me about his trip, waiting for his test results at the border, and the fact he saw a light on here last night. I remain cheerful, but my breakfast is going to burn if I don't tend to it. I'm in pyjamas, my hair in a wild knot. Jim's the kind of guy we all know, the bed-to-bed narrator: "I walked into the building and went up to the counter (describes the room), and I said, and then the woman said, then I said (every line of the dialogue), and then (full account of the test), and by the time I left, the rain started (weather report on the entire trip)." The stage whisper in my head grows louder as I turn off the stove, a stiff Jim Carrey grin still pasted on my face. Don't ask him in, don't say let me pour you a coffee.

I remind myself rural life isn't what it was in his day. People left doors unlocked and walked willy-nilly into one another's houses or workshops. It's only an essay; it's only breakfast. Decide what's important.

And yet. Like many writers, I am always fighting for privacy and when I can focus on my work any interruption throws me off. Now I worry this morning's smile didn't reach my eyes.

It was a long twenty minutes.

Patience can/should develop with age, true, but it seems to be more available the more experience we gain. When we've witnessed a vast range of responses and outcomes to writing-related circumstances, for example, the worry fuelling our impatience lessens. All the more reason to work on our fear. I learned to apply the "what's the worst that could happen?" check, along with its companion wrist-slap: "Oh, get over yourself." Even as adults, we have to be reminded to step out of our Piagetian ego bubble and understand where others are coming from. Artists are known for our thin skins and fragile egos. John Lennon once said, "Part of me suspects I am a loser and part of me thinks I am God Almighty." And Patrick Stump sang: "I don't care what you think as long as it's about me."[1]

When I escaped the world of academic writing at the age of fifty and began to write poetry, it felt as though I'd come home. My poetry was accepted in journals; I wrote an award-winning manuscript and entered a world of like-minded people. Pressure to keep moving and publish more intensified. I was on poetry tours (imagine) and the festival circuit and threw my heart into a four-year term as a poet laureate. Heady times.

One year, the poems stopped coming. Had I been spending so much of my time working, teaching, and performing in the poetry community I'd left no reflective time for writing? Or had the well run dry? "Don't worry," said a mentor. "We all have fallow periods. Wait it out." I resurrected a manuscript of lyric essays to revise them, but during that time Life Happened, Big Time: deaths and accidents and family health crises, moving house, fighting school administrators on behalf of a special needs son, developing a PhD program, the disruptions of an angry teenager, political dust-ups at work, you name it. The water in the well was rising again—I had plenty to write about—but now I struggled to find meditative time even to process the events, let alone put them in words. I began to realize writing comes when it comes and, for me, it comes in fits and starts. Do I wait for a muse? No. If there's a muse, they wear overalls. Writing is work. Or perhaps the muse is only a magical pairing of a clear head with the time and space to put it to use. In life and writing, I try to remember that winter, metaphorically and literally, is a time when what's dormant is only waiting to emerge.

A solitaire app is useful in airports. Wait to check in, wait at the gate, wait for the first-class fliers to board, wait for a seat partner to arrive, wait for the interminable announcements to be over. Stay occupied and alert at the same time. As a child, I played a well-worn deck of cards after I'd read my basketful of library books, sketched, painted, or spent the day wandering in the woods. Waiting to go back to school where I'd have to look! wait! ask! for permission to read the next gripping chapter in the lives of Dick and Jane.

In the same way, I putter when I'm waiting for the time to write or when I'm stuck. Housemates learn to recognize the middle-distance gaze of a writer who seems to be cleaning, fixing, sorting, or cooking. We may have abandoned the keyboard, but not the work. Puttering is patience in action.

Kierkegaard offers this thought: "Patience is not resignation, passivity, or inaction; rather it is the emergence of freedom within the domain where necessity rules."

Writing is both meditation and medication; it calms me, allows me to sort out what matters and what has meaning. Observations drop into a mental vat where they simmer and brew, seasoning how I think about an issue. My mind needs time to dig, to mull, to play with a thought from a number of perspectives. On occasion I can write quickly, cover the surface, but the kind of writing that grounds me is hard-won; it tests my assumptions and biases and tumbles me out on the last page, eager for more. Writing is thinking; it is movement. I can sit in a car for hours, imagining my trip, but unless I turn on the ignition, I'll never get out of the driveway.

Do poetry and lyrical nonfiction demand different cognitive processes than those of reportage or fiction or instruction manuals? Probably, but I don't know. The words of some talented writers pour from a gold-plated faucet of linguistic inspiration, whatever the genre. I have accepted it: I'm a plodder. The older I am, the more contemplative I've become. I wait. Revise. Wait some more.

Recently a person I worked with, a good writer, produced an essay a week and submitted each one immediately to a journal. "Hang on," I said. "Don't you want to let the piece settle, to give it some distance?" We may think that's the final draft, but the engine of our subconscious can still be humming with options. Soon after, the writer began to report on the rejections. *Clearly, I'm not cut out for writing essays.* So discouraged. Aside from the fact publishing decisions are made for many reasons other than quality (criteria for which can be subjective), we still have to give our work its best shot (*Patience, Grasshopper*). Our eagerness for a byline or a publication can sabotage us. The adage, "any port in a storm" can work when our life is at stake, but opting for publishing a less-than-ready piece with any outlet that will accept it, may, in time, feel hollow. Many of us have learned this the hard way (those early pieces of mine remain off my resumé).

Research Shows:
1. Patient people are more persistent and consistent in achieving goals. They are less likely to be quitters.
2. Patience begets patience, which increases a sense of well-being and accomplishment, which, in turn, provides more confidence to pursue more challenging goals.
3. We can train ourselves to be patient.
4. While patience is a sign of maturity, people differ in what they consider tolerable "wait times" and what conditions

try that patience (injustices, incompetence, danger, for example).

5. Patience is correlated with higher agreeableness, openness, and with lower neuroticism.[3]

The last decade or so I've been living a contradiction: the fewer years I have left, the more patience I've developed. Writing for writing's sake delivers me, composes me, perhaps even recreates me, over and over. I want to improve, to push myself, not to be distracted by a gerbil wheel of others' markers of success. Those markers vary, of course, from a publishing contract (large or small house or self-publishing) to thousands of social media followers, prizes, sales, or invitations to literary festivals and readings (notice I didn't mention a flourishing bank account). External success, to me, is a strong connection with readers, whether it's receiving mail about the work or an opportunity to have a chat about issues the writing poses. Writing is ultimately a conversation. That sounds more noble than it is, but it works for me, an introvert who tries daily to avoid the spotlight as much as possible.

And so, I curl up at home with my books and my keyboard, a tortoise among my writing friends. I wonder if learning patience over the years has given me a certain confidence to know what needs to be done, to consider possibilities rather than allow my ego to take charge and rush for rushing's sake. A quote by a woman named Anonymous reminds me that patience, after all, isn't weakness or passivity; it's a mark of strength and tolerance. I'm hoping she's right; my unfinished manuscript is at stake.

LORRI NEILSEN GLENN is the author and editor of a number of award-winning poetry, creative nonfiction, and scholarly titles. Halifax's first poet laureate of Red River Métis descent, she lives and teaches in Mi'kma'ki.

Conclusion

The irony is not lost on us.

We were beyond happy when this anthology got picked up by a traditional publisher, and of course we celebrated this success. As human beings raised and living in a world where achievement is measured in acclaim, recognition, and money, we are not immune to wanting what we've been programmed to want. Do we believe with all our hearts that art doesn't need to be commodified to be called art? Yes. Do we believe that those who create art have inherent value and that their work is essential—that they make the world better because of their art? Yes! This anthology, then, is needed more than ever. If we, the editors who wanted to open this discussion up—to explore why everyone with a crochet hook is asked if they're going to open an Etsy shop—if we acknowledge the thrill, the satisfaction, of having our work bought, then we've still got some capitalist dismantling to do, friends.

How, then, do we start? What do we need to do as a society to re-imagine the link between art and commerce? Is it possible to prize art beyond its monetary value and compensate artists fairly for their work? Sometimes these feel like impossible questions, but our essayists have helped us understand that art happens despite everything.

At the end of this anthology, it strikes us that these disparate voices speak one universal truth: art, creativity, the desire for beauty, and the ceaseless quest to understand the world's complexities are part of all of us. Perhaps it is the artists of the world (even when they eschew this label) who we trust to write the words of this truth, or paint of this truth, or sing of this truth. These voices are not isolated or fringe—they speak to the human condition, each essay a colourful thread in the tapestry of what gives life its meaning. And, although each voice is unique, together they are an intricate choral arrangement: resonant, immediate, urgent, and moving.

This collection, with apologies to Whitman, contains multitudes, each essay a testimony to the human longing for creation, whatever form it may take. When we, the editors, sat together eating delicious pastries and massaging this manuscript into order, we felt it. When each of us wrote our own contribution to this conversation, we felt it. We might not have understood fully at the beginning of this enterprise what we were trying to give voice to, but by the end, it became astonishingly clear: by trying to shoehorn art into a capitalist patriarchal structure, by splitting ourselves into two—one who must create and one who must earn—we lose ourselves and the world loses our art.

To be honest, we struggled to write our own essays. As the deadline sped toward us, we ramped up our text chain: "It's on the way, I swear." "I'll have it done by tomorrow night." Part of this was sheer workload; the deadline came as we were all mired in full-time demands, whether domestic, professional, or some horrendous combination of the two. But as we started writing the essays, we realized, one by one, the real reason we'd procrastinated. We hadn't been willing to acknowledge our own relationships to our art and the deep excavation we faced threatened to turn us inside out. The text chain quickly turned to choruses of "I'm sorry," "I think this might be bad," "I cried the whole time I wrote it." None of us expected to be as personal as we were.

We all function as teachers and leaders in our respective professional worlds. Day after day, we offer guidance, based on the supposed wisdom we've gathered and shaped into nuggets of advice to hand out to our students and mentees. Coming together in our weekly meetings, we'll confess to not having got our creative work done, but not in a way that belies our vulnerability around it. Encouragement peppers our chats; we cheer each other on and rarely open up to feeling like failures because we haven't written the piece, made the thing. When it came time to write our essays for this book, we had to face those feelings head-on. No wonder we struggled.

Stepping permanently outside of a roiling productivity soup will take more than occasional segments of artmaking time, marked by furious typing and a box of Kleenex. We also can't really reject productivity culture as we hand you this tangible thing to buy and read, to comment on and take up real estate on your shelf. We are grateful for our editor and publisher and distributor, the bookstores and media who have helped us get this out into the world. So instead of questioning this product for its very nature, we honour all those who stepped in, whose mark, however slight, made this book. It comes to you as we quiet screaming children, answer emails, nurse our pain, calm our minds. We found our way around the machine to make something together. It took us nearly four years, but what does that matter in a lifetime of making art?

Acknowledgements

We would like to thank all those at TouchWood Editions/Brindle & Glass who helped us bring this book into the world. Thanks to Tori Elliott for understanding our vision, to Kate Kennedy for your editorial guidance, Senica Maltese for your much-appreciated copy-editor's eye, and Curtis Samuel for your guidance and expertise.

We'd be remiss not to thank our community of fellow writers, many of whom we've met through the University of King's College MFA program.

Thanks to all our contributors for such thoughtful, brilliant ruminations on creativity. When we put the call out, we did not expect such a flurry of responses, nor the breadth and depth of them. Their essays remind us that we're not alone in our messy, unproductive creativity, and we must remember to turn to community when the words stop flowing.

NELLWYN'S ACKNOWLEDGEMENTS: Thank you to my parents for the first universal truth, and to my entire extended family for supporting my creative endeavours. To Nathan, for loving me as I am and helping me grow.

My work is infinitely more joyful (and easier!) thanks to the incredible King's College community and my wonderful colleagues at Another Story Bookshop. Huge thanks, always, to my agent

Hilary McMahon and the team at Westwood Creative Artists, whose support is multifaceted and unwavering.

I am grateful to have had more than my fair share of life-changing teachers, but this book, in particular, is for Carolyn Wren.

PAMELA'S ACKNOWLEDGMENTS: To the friends who have supported me through the thick and thin, and those who patiently listened as I read my scribbles over the years, the CAPA gals, Mary, Karla, Derrick, Patz, Veronica, and Anne. To my parents for showing me what it means to keep on keeping on. And to my family: My husband Mark for his support in all the ways, to my two boys, Charlie and Harris, without whom I would be a lesser version of me, and of course, Nellwyn the dog for taking me for long walks and reminding me that everything in life can be made better with snacks and naps.

CHRISTIAN'S ACKNOWLEDGMENTS: I am deeply grateful for the opportunity to collaborate with an outstanding publisher and my exceptionally talented co-editors. I extend special thanks to Vandan Arora for his unwavering support and understanding during the times when I needed to immerse myself fully in *Bad Artist* and other creative projects. Despite life's distractions and tempting diversions, Vandan stood by me, allowing me to close my office door and give my undivided attention to *Bad Artist*. I am profoundly thankful to my father, Kevan Smith, for his continuous encouragement and belief in my creative pursuits. My father's sense of humour and optimistic perspective on life serve as a constant source of inspiration for me.

GILLIAN'S ACKNOWLEDGMENTS: Thanks to my colleagues, especially all the King's MFA Faculty Mentors, and Stephen Kimber, Kim Pittaway, Dean Jobb, and Charlotte Gill for your brilliance and inspiration. To Louise Wrazen: Life will never be the same without our conversations. I miss you every day. To my fellow creators and friends, all of whom show me there is no one way to be an artist. To my parents and brothers: you are all first and foremost artists. Thanks to my sisters Helen, Shannon, and Rachel, my parents-in-law Donna and Brian, and my nephew Vince. I love you all. And to my tiny family: Emily, Martie, Geddy, and my number one artist, Pete. May we continue to create gardens, games, good snacks, happy times, and love together.

Notes

"I'm So Lazy, I Can't Stop Crying" by Gillian Turnbull

1. Susan George, "A Short History of Neoliberalism," *Transnational Institute*, March 24, 1999, https://www.tni.org/en/article/a-short-history-of-neoliberalism.

2. Jamie Peck and Adam Tickell, "Jungle Law Breaks Out: Neoliberalism and Global-Local Disorder," *The Royal Geographical Society* 26, no. 4 (January 1994), 317–326.

3. Luca Katzenmajer-Pump, Dániel Komáromy, and Judit Balázs, "The Importance of Recognizing Worthlessness for Suicide Pevention in Adolescents with Attention-Deficit/Hyperactivity Disorder," *Front Psychiatry* (November 15, 2022), DOI: 10.3389/fpsyt.2022.969164.

4. Jon Pareles, "Taking Himself Out of the Equation: Sting Lets Other Voices Sing in a Show About Shipyards," *The New York Times*, September 15, 2013.

5. Emma Brockes, "Sting's Tale," *The Guardian*, November 12, 2003, https://www.theguardian.com/music/2003/nov/12/biography.popandrock.

6. "Steven Soderbergh on His Year in Reading," January 12, 2024, in *The New York Times Book Review* Podcast, https://www.nytimes.com/2024/01/12/books/review/steven-soderberghs-year-in-reading.html.

"In Defence of Giving Up" by Stacey May Fowles

1. Brianna Wiest, "'Permalancing' Is the New Self-Employment Trend You'll Be Seeing Everywhere," *Forbes Magazine*, June 14, 2018, www.forbes.com/sites/briannawiest/2018/06/13/permalancing -is-the-new-self-employment-trend-youll-be-seeing-everywhere /?sh=65732293a383.

"Betrayal: The Bad Artist's Greatest Act" by Nicola Perry
1. Gayatri Naraine, "The Feminine Principle," in *The Fabric of the Future: Women Visionaries Illuminate the Path to Tomorrow*, ed. M.J. Ryan (Berkeley: Conari Press, 1998).
2. Akina Alholm, "When less is more," *The New Indian Express,* October 13, 2023, https://www.newindianexpress.com/lifestyle/spirituality /2023/Oct/14/when-less-is-more-2623317.html.

"The Murakami Method: Rewriting Long Covid" by Linda Browne
1. Audre Lorde, "The Uses of the Erotic: The Erotic as Power," in *Sister Outsider* (New York: Penguin Random House, 2007).
2. Mary Hynes (Host), "Lessons From a War Zone: How to Emotionally Survive and Flourish in the Pandemic," April 18, 2021, in *Tapestry* podcast, https://www.cbc.ca/listen/live-radio/1-59-tapestry /clip/15837710-lessons-war-zone.
3. *The Great British Bake Off*, season 6, episode 10, "The Final," aired October 7, 2015, on cbc, https://gem.cbc.ca/the-great-british -baking-show/s06?autoplay=1.
4. Lorde, "The Uses of the Erotic: The Erotic as Power."

"Writing as an ADHDer" by Jess Mannion
1. Thomas E. Brown, *A New Understanding of ADHD in Children and Adults* (New York: Routledge, 2013).
2. via Institute on Character (website), accessed March 2024, https://www.viacharacter.org/.
3. Francesco Cirillo, *The Pomodoro Technique: The Life-Changing Time-Management System* (London: Virgin Books, 2018).

"More Like a Garden" by Jessica Payne
1. Delcy Morelos, *El Abrazo* (New York: Dia Chelsea, October 5, 2023 – July 20, 2024), exhibition brochure, https://www.diaart.org /exhibition/exhibitions-projects/delcy-morelos-el-abrazo-exhibition.
2. George Orwell, "Why I Write," *Gangrel* no. 4 (Summer 1946), https:// www.orwellfoundation.com/the-orwell-foundation/orwell /essays-and-other-works/why-i-write/.
3. Ann Patchett, "The Getaway Car: A Practical Memoir about Writing and Life," in *This Is The Story Of A Happy Marriage.* (New York: Harper-Collins. 2013), 19–60.
4. Patchett, "Getaway Car," 31–32.

5. Thora Siemsen, "On Being Vulnerable in Your Work: An Interview with Writer Sheila Heti," *The Creative Independent*, May 22, 2018, https://thecreativeindependent.com/people/author-sheila-heti -on-being-vulnerable-in-your-work/.

6. Natalia Ginzburg, "My Vocation," in *The Little Virtues*, trans. Dick Davis (New York: Arcade Publishing, 1962), 66.

"Gross Domestic Productivity" by Pamela Oakley

1. *The Bear*, season 2, episode 14, "Fishes," directed by Christopher Storer, written by Joanna Calo and Christopher Storer, aired June 22, 2023, on Disney+.

2. Virginia Woolf, "Professions for Women," in *The Death of the Moth, and Other Essays* (London: Hogarth Press, 1942), 235–242.

"How Can You Write Poetry If You Don't Go Outside?" by Anna Lee-Popham

1. Adrienne Rich, "Motherhood and Daughterhood," in *Essential Essays: Culture, Politics, and the Art of Poetry* (New York: W.W. Norton, 2018), 112.

2. Paulo Freire, "I've Always Been Ambivalent About Charismatic Leaders," in *We Make the Road by Walking: Conversations on Education and Social Change*, edited by Paulo Freire and Myles Horton (Philadelphia: Temple University Press, 1990), 109–114.

3. Aleksandar Hemon, quoted in Richard Lea, "Fiction v Nonfiction: English Literature's Made-up Divide," *The Guardian*, March 24, 2016, https:// www.theguardian.com/books/2016/mar/24/fiction-nonfiction -english-literature-culture-writers-other-languages-stories.

4. Adrienne Rich, "The Burning of Paper Instead of Children," *The Will to Change*, (New York: W.W. Norton, 1971). 15.

5. Dhruv Jani, "The Concentric Fictions of a Generous History: Hypertext and Other Annotations to Memory," *Thinking Spaces: The Reading Group and Speaker Series* (University of Guelph, March 26, 2021).

"Creating Outside the Boxes" by Wanda Taylor

1. Ann Pietrangelo, "Left Brain vs Right Brain: What Does This Mean for Me?," *Healthline*, February 5, 2024, https://www.healthline.com /health/left-brain-vs-right-brain.

2. Robert H. Shmerling, "Right Brain/Left Brain, Right?" *Harvard Health*, March 24, 2022, https://www.health.harvard.edu/blog/right-brain left-brain-right-2017082512222.

"Turning Down Syndrome into Art" by Adelle Purdham
1. Sheila Heti, *How Should a Person Be?* (Toronto: House of Anansi Press, 2014), 114.
2. Erin Wunker, *Notes from a Feminist Killjoy* (Toronto: Book*hug Press, 2016), 160–161.
3. Heather Lanier, *Raising A Rare Girl: A Memoir* (New York: Penguin Press, 2020), 120.
4. Alicia Elliott, *A Mind Spread Out on the Ground* (Toronto: Anchor Canada, 2020).
5. Eula Biss, *On Immunity: An Inoculation* (Minneapolis, Minnesota: Greywolf Press, 2014), 117.
6. "Ernest M. Hemmingway," The Poetry Foundation (website), accessed March 2024, https://www.poetryfoundation.org/poets/ernest-m-hemingway.
7. Audre Lorde, "Age, Race, Class, and Sex: Women Redefining Difference," in *Sister Outsider* (New York: Random House, 2007), 115.
8. Wendell Berry, *The Country of Marriage* (California: Counterpoint, 2013), 8.

"Hummingbird" by Gloria Blizzard
1. Alexxa Gotthardt, "How to Be an Artist, According to Georgia O'Keefe," *Artsy,* March 11, 2018, https://www.artsy.net/article/artsy-editorial-artist-georgia-okeeffe.

"How I Stay Creative While Working My Ass Off (For Someone Else's Art)" by Set L. Shuter
1. Elizabeth Gilbert, *Big Magic* (New York: Riverhead Books, 2016), 138.
2. John Cleese, *Creativity: A Short and Cheerful Guide* (London: Hutchinson, 2020), 59.

"Field Notes on Patience (in Shreds)" by Lorri Neilsen Glenn
1. David Sheff, *All We Are Saying: The Last Major Interview with John Lennon and Yoko Ono* (New York: St. Martin's Press, 2020), 195.
2. Ralph L. Piedmont, ed., *Research in the Social Scientific Study of Religion, Volume 10,* (Maryland: Loyola College, 2007), 179.
3. Sarah A. Schnitker, "An Examination of Patience and Well-Being," *The Journal of Positive Psychology* 7, no. 4 (2012): 263–280.

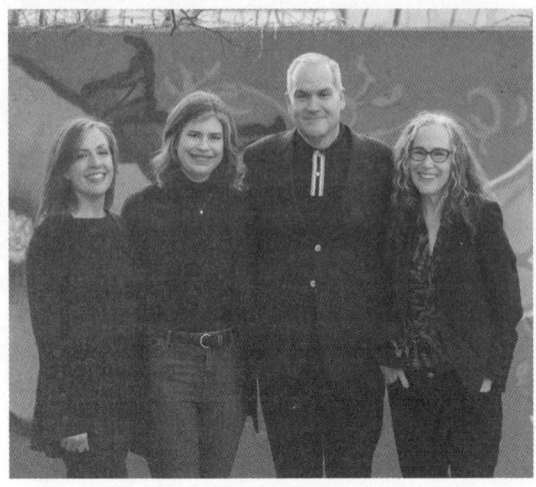

IMAGE BY PAUL LAMBERT

Nellwyn, Pamela, Christian, and Gillian met and formed a writing group during their MFA in Creative Nonfiction at the University of King's College, Halifax. For nearly a decade, the group has supported, encouraged, and adored each other and each other's work. This anthology stands as tribute to their unique relationship and collaborative gifts. In the spirit of this collection, they are self-proclaimed Bad Artists showing the world that beautiful things can still be made despite obstacles, naysayers, and endless to-do lists.